Marguerite Wolff, Adventures of a Concert Pianist

by Robert Clarson-Leach

Book Reviews and Appraisals

BOOK OF THE WEEK, Yorkshire Evening Post. 'Marguerite grew up to play in jails and jungle locations as well as the world's greatest halls and salons and embassies of Europe.' *Jim Greenfield.*

'*The YEP's review is fabulous — congratulations.*'
Vivian Stuart. Author, **The Australians,** (USA sales over 5 million).

'It is a unique story . . . the moments of tragedy that have shadowed Miss Wolff's life (thankfully outnumbered by more happy events) are revealed with admirable candour . . . and with the stamp of unassailable authority which informs the fluently-written pages of this intriguing volume.'
Robert Matthew-Walker, Editor, **Music and Musicians.**

'Here she tells of her passion for music and the story of her comeback (following the death of her husband) . . . She has received the additional accolade of having her biography published, written by Robert Clarson-Leach.' *Sally Brompton.* **The Times.**

'The first thing to say is how enthrallingly written it is . . . she could not have found a better biographer.'
Keith Fagan. **The Liszt Society.**

'She lives in an elegant London home in Belgravia with three Steinway pianos dotted around the house.'
Shirley Davenport. **Evening Gazette.**

'She wears a new Hartnell dress for the launching of her biography.' *Nigel Dempster.* **The Daily Mail.**

'Marguerite Wolff might be described as incident prone . . . a chance meeting in prison led to her biography . . . the book jacket picture was taken, naturally, by Snowdon.'
Chronicler. **The Jewish Chronicle.**

'A wonderfully gossipy chapter on clothes . . . the book comes surprisingly up to date with the Dikko affair and Mrs. Gandhi's assassination.' *Leonard Pearcey.* **Classical Music.**

'Piano playing can lead to some strange situations.' *Shirley Davenport.* **The Yorkshire Post.**

'She turned to Solomon for a wider view of music . . . she found that Kentner's tuition was exhilarating. Marguerite's story is full of the expected chatter of the artist's room in concert halls around the world. Always slim and elegant she has many admirers in music, art and diplomacy.'
E. Alan Smith. **The Daily Telegraph.**

'There's many a so-called "best-selling" author would like to have reviews like these!'.
Diane Pearson. Author, **Csardas,** etc.

'I congratulate you on the prodigious impact which the book has made on the public, and not only on the musical world: that is a triumph these days.' *Charles Cleall.* **Composer.**

'What a charming present!' *The Lady Diana Cooper.*

MARGUERITE WOLFF

adventures of a concert pianist

Robert Clarson-Leach

ARTMUSIQUE PUBLISHING Co.
31 Perry Hill,
London SE6 4LF.

First Published in U.K., March, 1985, by
ARTMUSIQUE PUBLISHING Co.
31 Perry Hill,
London SE6 4LF.

ISBN 0 946444 01 3

The author apologises to the many people who should have been mentioned in
this book but have been omitted. The selection has been mine. Marguerite
would have wished for more but there have been two limiting factors: space,
and the need to keep the story flowing.

R.C-L.

Every endeavour has been made to correctly spell names of people and places.
However, in some cases it has not been possible to obtain authoritive
confirmation. Any name which is mis-spelt and brought to the attention of the
author will be corrected in subsequent editions. (Chopin was giving a recital in
Paris and he noticed that his name was given in the programme as 'Shoppin'.)

Copyright permission for use of photographs has in all known instances been
applied for. In looking through the personal effects of Marguerite Wolff the
author has come across photographs with no copyright details on the reverse
side. These have been used in good faith. Any inadvertent mis-use of copyright
will be immediately rectified by formal application once it is brought to the
notice of the author.

Book Jacket. Correction.
MARGUERITE WOLFF.
Lines 28 and 29.
'works of Sir Arthur Bliss who has composed music specially for her. Marguerite made'
these lines should read,
'works of Sir Arthur Bliss who dedicated one of his works to her. Marguerite made'

design/print Thanet Printing Works Ltd., 81 High Street, Ramsgate, Kent.

Acknowledgements

Grateful acknowledgements are due to those who have spent time reading, and making corrections to, the typescript; Marguerite's sister Dolly, my wife Daphne, Robert Leach (Technical Editor of *The Accountant*), and Stan Wyatt (Thanet Printing Works).

Members of Marguerite's family, and several people close to her, have spoken or written to me, supplying information and views used in this book; daughters Crystal and Gloria, sister Dolly, Nat Kofsky, Anna Schouvaloff, Wim Hemmink, Robert Glazebrook (Steinway Pianos), John Walsh, Norman Hartnell Co. Ltd., Eunice Mistarz (The Liszt Society).

Copyright permission has been applied for wherever required and credited on the appropriate page. Special thanks are due to Lady Bliss for reading and making corrections to Chapter 5. Lord Snowdon gave permission for the front cover picture, and Novello and Co., with Lady Bliss, permitted reproduction of part of the Arthur Bliss *Piano Sonata*. Thanks are due to the Press; The Daily Telegraph, The Press Association, Associated Press Ltd., The Times.

Thanks are also due to Martin Walford, solicitor, for legal and business advice, and for acting on Marguerite Wolff's behalf.

For Marguerite's parents,
Walter and Nina

Contents

Introduction   7

One   11

Two   25

Three   43

Four   59

Five   82

Six   100

Seven   116

Index   135

Introduction

MARGUERITE WOLFF
Adventures of a concert pianist

The desire to write a biography about Marguerite was immediate when I met her recently after a long period of time. The title of the book was no problem. However, the subtitle gave much food for thought and it was some time before *Adventures of a Concert Pianist* was decided upon.

Why 'adventures?' . . . because the word covers so many types of experience.

André Maurois, writing of the music of Mozart, uses the word in its aesthetic and intellectual senses:—

'Go to a concert; listen to those pure notes and those enchanting harmonies, and if your love then seems confused, harsh, and discordant, you are still unversed in the art of loving. But if, in your emotion, you are aware of this gradual acquisition of beauty, this marvellous understanding, this sublime reconciliation of conflicting and hostile themes beyond all dissonance, then you are embarked upon one of the few *adventures* in life that are worth having: a great love.'

(italics mine, R. C-L.)

The word 'adventure' is, of course, not only a noun (daring enterprise, unexpected or excited incident) but also a verb (to dare to go or come, to dare to enter, to hazard, or, to commit oneself).

In Shakespeare's *Romeo and Juliet,* when the heroine is on her balcony and fears for her lover's safety, she warns him, 'If they do see thee, they will murder thee!', but Romeo gallantly assures Juliet that he would cross the world just to see her, boldly declaring, '. . . wert thou as far as that vast shore washed with the farthest sea, I should *adventure* for such merchandise'.

(italics not Shakespeare's. R. C-L.)

7

'Adventure' is not necessarily swashbuckling or romantic heroics, however. Delicacy and accomplished skill can sway the balance between success and failure in many an adventure. As Ashley Dukes writes in *The Man with a Load of Mischief,* '*Adventure* must be held in delicate fingers. It should be handled, not embraced. It should be sipped not swallowed at a gulp'.

And from Milton's *Paradise Lost Bk. X,* can we not glimpse the expectancy of the audience awaiting the return of the concert pianist from her travels overseas?; '. . . and now expecting each hour their great *adventurer,* from the search of foreign worlds.'

Marguerite Wolff is ever travelling the globe, playing to audiences of foreign worlds and then, like Milton's 'great adventurer', returning to her home supporters in London, and the familiar pattern of concerts, practice and study.

The events in such a life-style as Marguerite Wolff's surely merit the title, 'adventures'.

Adventures excite not only the participants, but all those who hear or read about them; the preparation, the journeying, the entry into the unknown, the unexpected, the tragic and the triumphant, the colour and the glamour of famous places and interesting faces, the discovery of new art forms, new friends, new relationships, new ideas . . . all these 'adventures' have come the way of Marguerite because of her career as an international concert pianist.

An adventure story which is not fiction, but fact, is especially exciting because it is a *real* story, and the reader can relate himself to it. Such a story is a report on a real person, and this can make compulsive reading. It is a narrative of life, a small piece of history.

It can also be inspirational. What student does not tire of endless practice and study? How many students have not paused and asked themselves, 'is it worth it?'. 'where is it leading?', 'what is the end product?'. The way ahead seems blocked. Sometimes someone will come along with a helping hand, sometimes someone will clean a pane of darkened glass so that the student can see what lies ahead . . . but that is only sometimes. The essential ingredient is one's own determination. Whether in art, sport, industry, or learning of any kind, one's own determination is the only permanent factor. It is the only factor over which the person has some control.

That is why biographies can be so helpful and inspiring. We cannot only read of someone having this personal determination, we can also discover the answers to the questions which assail the tyro when the spirit is low, the 'is it worth it?' type of self-searching doubt. A biography can excitingly show that it *is* worth it. All the hard work, the initial loneliness and the early grind, these things do 'bring their reward. They make one's whole life an adventure. They make possible the life-style wherein adventures are possible. There is also a certain 'eternity' for the adventurer. One does not retire at 65, or 60, or any other arbitary age. As long as there is life, the adventures can continue.

The reasons for writing this book are, therefore, two-fold. The reader can enjoy learning of the adventures experienced by the artist and, in cases of self-doubt, the reader can gain inspiration from this 'success story'. The book can show one that the adventures of life are there for those who go to the trouble of making suitable preparation. One does not have to be the greatest artist in the world, the greatest athlete, the greatest industrialist, or the greatest anything . . . one only has truly to get the best out of oneself. Do that . . . and life becomes an adventure.

I met Marguerite Wolff quite late in my life but at a time when she was the youngest professor at Trinity College of Music, London. She was my piano teacher for three years. Marguerite wrote a testimonial which helped me gain my first teaching post (General Subjects; with special responsibility for Music and Games) in Richmond, Surrey.

The London County Council (later called 'The Inner London Education Authority', I.L.E.A.) also engaged me as a lecturer in music, and one of my weekly classes was at Wormwood Scrubs prison, West London. This lecture was given each Wednesday evening in the prison chapel, and I used the old 78 records plus the grand piano given to the prison by former inmate, Ivor Novello, to illustrate my talks. It was in this capacity that I met Marguerite Wolff again, because she was giving a piano recital in the main recreation hall of the prison. Instead of giving my captive audience their weekly talk on music we went to hear live music from Marguerite.

Marguerite very graciously agreed to add to her programme Brahms' *Rhapsody Op. 79 No. 2* at the special request of my 'Musical Appreciation' class, and this pleased them immensely.

The next time I met Marguerite several years had passed and I had deserted music for full-time writing. Marguerite had moved to a new and very exquisite new home, Chandos House, Belgravia, a mere stone's throw from the garden wall of Buckingham Palace. Marguerite gave a delightful house-warming party and it was there, as we exchanged news, that it came to me that it would be a marvellous idea to write a book about her adventures in music. I had spent most of my life lecturing and writing about musicians who were no longer with

Entering the prison gates to give a recital in the main recreation hall.

9

us. Why not a book on a musician who is very much alive, and very much with us?

I wrote to Marguerite, explaining why I wanted to write this book, and to my great joy she agreed to work with me on the project.

We spent many hours talking, all of it tape-recorded, and we dived into what Press cuttings still existed (Marguerite is very modest and did not keep all the Press notices she should have done, especially those from abroad), and I contacted, and sometimes interviewed, many of the personalities who have played a part in her adventures. This material was put together and Marguerite spent a lot of time going through the script with me.

The book was written, illustrated, edited, printed and launched within one year, half the time I usually need to write a biography, But then, Marguerite Wolff is alive, and was willing to give me a great deal of time-saving assistance.

It has been a pleasure working on the book and I hope readers will enjoy the fruits of this labour.

Robert Clarson-Leach. London 1985.

One

'Marguerite *will* be a concert pianist.'

Eight-year old Marguerite Wolff was too young to appreciate the full significance of what her music teacher, Mr. Barron, was telling her mother. There had been an emphasis on the word 'will' and Marguerite's mother must have been impressed by the sincerity of the piano teacher's words. Marguerite, herself, simply remembers the incident as one in a progression of steps leading her quite naturally into an adult life of professional piano playing.

Music was a way of life for Marguerite's family. Her mother was an excellent pianist, and her father was an equally good violinist. They played piano/violin duets.

Nina

The children; Marguerite, her younger sister Dolly (Dorothy), and two elder brothers Adolph and Arthur, were all taught the piano at home, and each child reached a very high standard of performance at an early age. The big passion in the life of the household was music.

Marguerite says, 'my mother told me she was playing the piano two hours before I was born!'

The family did not possess a wireless until long after everybody else had one. Marguerite's parents considered that it would inhibit their own live music-making. By the same token, when television sets began to appear in British homes Marguerite's parents considered that such a contraption would distract the children from reading and practising.

Patriotism was strong in the family, however, and, as there was a passionate desire to see the Queen's Coronation, a T.V. set was duly bought. The arrival of the television set did nothing to diminish the family's love of making music in the home. When they were not making music the parents loved to sit quietly and read. Marguerite's mother was a romantic and would bring home from the library the full quota of six novels at a time. Her father was a non-fiction reader, preferring biographies, histories, and editorials.

Nina, Marguerite's mother, was born in Hull, Yorkshire, and in 1911 she married her childhood sweetheart, Walter. Later they moved to London.

They were happily married for sixty-four years and, so close were they, that when Walter died in 1975 Nina passed on a mere seventeen days later. Their marriage had been a truly beautiful

11

love affair, and this created a secure and settled family base on which the four children could develop their talents and personalities.

The two boys shared a healthy interest in sport; rugby in the winter and cricket in the summer. They also loved flying, enlisting in the RAF, where Adolph became a Wing Commander and his younger brother, Arthur, a Flying Officer. Tragically, Arthur was killed on active service with the RAF. He looked to have a brilliant career in law, having gained his LL.B. degree when only nineteen.

He was an excellent pianist and many consider that had he chosen a career in music his playing could have equalled that of Marguerite and Dolly. Adolph, who as a law student spent his lunch money on flying lessons, became a distinguished lawyer after he qualified.

Marguerite, too, was caught up in the flying craze. When she was twelve the famous flying ace, Nigel Tangye, husband of film actress Ann Todd, took Marguerite aloft for a spin. Her brothers were 'in' on the escapade but the older and more sedate members of the family were less than pleased. One aunt, known for her Victorian-like prejudices, was quite outspoken, 'Oh!, the deceit of it! the deceit of it!'

In adult life Marguerite retained her love of flying, being able to use this form of transport for her many overseas tours as a concert pianist. By contrast, she hates earth-bound traffic and has never bothered to learn to drive a car.

'I love being up in the air!' she says, sharing her brothers' love of flying. Unfortunately, she was not allowed to become a post-war Amy Johnson or Amelia Earhart, so it was 'back to the piano keyboard'.

Her sister Dolly also entered the professional world of piano playing. However, a personal tragedy in Dolly's private life interrupted what was beginning to look like a very promising performing career in music.

So it was left, at least at that time, to Marguerite to carry the family honour on to the concert platform.

As far back as she can remember it seemed to be the natural thing for her to learn to play the piano. Other girls might learn to knit, or cook, but for Marguerite her natural proclivity was music. At the age of five she was competent. Her mother was teaching her in those early years. When Marguerite was about eight Nina decided that an outside teacher should be employed and Marguerite remembers her mother saying that she was bringing a Mr. Barron into the house to continue the piano lessons.

Walter, as a young man.

12

Adolph

Arthur

He was a kindly yet impressive-looking man, and at the piano he could improvise marvellously. After each lesson Marguerite would ask him to display his keyboard skill, and this remains more clearly in her memory than the actual lessons. It was after about the third lesson that Mr. Barron made the afore-mentioned vitally significant remark to Nina, 'Marguerite *will* be a concert pianist.'

This did not come as a surprise to the little girl. She did not know fully what it meant. If people came to the house Marguerite always enjoyed playing to them. She always wanted to play to people, and if she got the chance at school she would also play there. Marguerite remembers that Mr. Barron's statement made her mother look pleased, but the matter was not discussed in her presence. Any discussion that took place would have been between Nina and Walter and it seems, in retrospect, that the parents were happy to accept Mr. Barron's assessment of Marguerite's potential, and see what developed in her lessons. The family then seemed to take it for granted that Marguerite would be a concert pianist one day. Even so, it did not affect the family life in any way, and the pattern of practice did not change. Marguerite was far too young to begin seriously planning her own future and decisions were made for her by her parents as in all other households where parents want the best careers for their young children.

Marguerite

Dolly

The only visible sign that Mr. Barron's statement had made an impact was the vigilance with which Nina now supervised her daughter's practice. It was, though, Marguerite's own driving passion for music which led her to the piano as soon as she arrived home from school, but now her mother would patiently and attentively sit by the piano while her daughter practised. Marguerite did not feel that the pattern of her life was in anyway altered. Her parents were obviously thinking about her future, but it was not discussed in front of her.

The form of Marguerite's piano lessons did not change for several years. There were times when her natural high spirits made her rebel a little at the regularity and discipline of daily practice, so her mother would wisely advise her to go out for a walk, but with this clever proviso, 'Yes, go out, darling. It will do you good, and it will make you even fresher for your work when you return!'

Thus, the desire to go out and play was duly followed by the desire to return home and practise.

There were usually two pianos going at home and frequently Marguerite and Dolly would play duets. Dolly, even at the age of three, had demanded to be taught the piano by her mother, so Mr. Barron also gave lessons to Marguerite's younger sister.

14

To give some indication of Dolly's ability it is worth recording that she played at the Wigmore Hall when she was seven (Sir Henry Wood being tremendously impressed), and when she was ten she played the Beethoven *C Major Concerto* in London, Walter Legge of HMV saying that she had the biggest talent in Europe.

Walter Legge was not one to give praise freely. At the time that he first heard Dolly play, that is, before the Beethoven *C Major Concerto* performance, he was married to the very beautiful mezzo-soprano, Nancy Evans, who achieved fame singing the notoriously difficult part of *The Merry Widow,* and was first to sing the part of 'Lucretia' for The English Opera Group. But even the charm of Nancy seemingly did not sweeten the caustic tongue of Walter. He remained a man who said what he thought.

A young singer had been auditioned before Dolly was due to play. Legge stopped the singer with a devastating comment, 'Do you mind? . . . this is one of my favourite songs.'

The shattered singer crept off-stage and Dolly was only encouraged to present herself when Legge softened, turned to her, and said, 'Come along. Now we shall have some music!'

At Trinity College of Music Dolly gained a Senior Scholarship at an extremely early age and it was partly through a joke played at the right time and with the right professor that her talent was noted.

The well-known violinist Izzy (Israel) Aaronovitch liked practising with Dolly at the piano, and Nina had a private recording made of Dolly's piano playing. Izzy was listening to it in the college library when the cellist, Ludwig Lebell, a much-respected professor at the college, entered. Dolly was present.

'Myra Hess,' said Izzy, nodding towards the gramophone.

When the record finished Ludwig praised the performance of the famous Myra, only for Izzy to laugh and confess that the recording had been made by Dolly.

Ludwig, a great character himself, took the joke well and the incident played a big part in Dolly's being considered for, and granted, the scholarship.

For the present, however, she plays a much appreciated role in supporting Marguerite at concerts. She sits in the Artists' Room with her elder sister, kisses her 'Goodbye' before the grand entrance, and Marguerite, sometimes feeling as if she is going to the guillotine, is immensely happy to have Dolly there to see her off, and welcome her back when the performance is over. Throughout the whole of their lives the two sisters have been extremely close, and a source of strength to each other on many occasions.

Remembering their childhood Dolly says of Marguerite, 'She was the most loving sister in the whole world. I don't think there is another one like her. In my earliest days her interest in me was immense. Now I can see how rare it was.'

Marguerite's brother, the lawyer, is devoted in a more masculinely offhand way. He will ring Marguerite after a concert and tell her that she played 'reasonably well', but it is not so much what big brother said, the important thing is that he was there and telephoned his congratulations, albeit in brotherly under-statement.

Marguerite, a believer in exercising both mind and body, studied ballet with Ivy Bell. Ivy was one of several who, knowing that Marguerite was destined for the concert platform, felt that there was something lacking in the progress Marguerite was making. Thomas Knott, a professor of piano at The Royal Academy, was Ivy Bell's father-in-law and it was arranged that he should hear Marguerite play.

The outcome of this was a parental decision that Marguerite should continue to enjoy her ballet lessons with Ivy, but that a more serious application be given to her piano studies. This was put tactfully to Mr. Barron who readily agreed that it would be very much to Marguerite's benefit if she attended The Royal Academy of Music and studied with Thomas Knott.

Things went well for a number of years but the time came when Nina and Walter felt that there ought to be something more. There was no concentration on any one aspect, and there did not seem to be any significant advance in technique.

The doubts were not something that could be put into words. These doubts were instinctive.

At that time there were three piano teachers who were known for producing talented young pianists.

One was Mabel Landau, who taught the Royal children.

Another was a Russian, Madame Levinskaya. Marguerite remembers her as 'a vast lady, with a thunderous personality, who wore black velvet with white fox all the way round'. 'I remember it vividly,' says Marguerite.

The third was Gertrude Azulay.

Marguerite was taken to concerts given by the pupils of Mabel Landau, and of Levinskaya, with a view to her going to study with one or the other.

While a choice was being considered, a neighbour met Marguerite's mother and insisted that Gertrude Azulay was the teacher for Marguerite (and Dolly, too, because both girls were now showing extreme promise and both were keen to become professional pianists).

'Gertrude Azulay is so meticulous, so careful, . . .' enthused the neighbour, and Nina thought that the least she could do was march her two daughters off to see what this third teacher had to offer.

Marguerite's meeting with Gertrude Azulay was traumatic. It was, to say the least, a startling meeting which remained forever as a sharply defined vignette in Marguerite's memory, and for Dolly . . . an encounter which severely jolted her usually serene nervous system.

For the two girls, their life as piano students had been success and praise all the way. Marguerite had passed a very stiff piano examination and * Gordon Jacob had added to his praise the statement, 'Well, obviously you are going to have a concert career', and Marguerite had replied with a respectful but confident, 'Yes'. Other important experts had picked her out as a future concert pianist; William Murdoch, Howard Jones . . . it was an accepted thing that Marguerite was going to be a pianist and, indeed, she was already giving public concerts despite her tender age.

Then this day arrived when the confident little pianist had to play for her prospective teacher, Gertrude Azulay.

Marguerite got as far as the second or third bar.

'S-S-Stop! It is really . . . very bad!'

Marguerite, Dolly and Nina could hardly believe their ears. No one had ever spoken to Marguerite like that.

Marguerite's mother, however, with true Yorkshire common sense, had never been impressed by false praise, and even though she had become used to the most important of people in the profession stating how promising her daughter's playing was, she was willing to give credence to this Azulay lady. In the heavy silence following the teacher's outburst Nina was thinking hard.

Had she not 'felt' that progress was not quite right? Had she, therefore, been led to this Gertrude Azulay by instinct? Was this tough teacher the one to lead Marguerite towards the hard world of professional music?

Marguerite, for her part, remembers the incident as the ending of the gloriously naive years and the beginning of a new road, a hard and realistic one.

*Gordon Jacob, an authority on orchestration, wrote the ballet 'Uncle Remus', and much light-hearted music for the B.B.C. radio programme ITMA (comedy).

Gertrude Azulay, it is believed, was born in England, and was of Jewish Sephardi stock, a high Jewish sect who pride themselves that they are of aristocratic origins, usually Spanish or Portuguese.

She was of that strong type of personality which automatically led her to believe that if she said she would take a young pupil, then the parents would feel honoured and there would be no question of 'dithering' or 'thinking about it'.

Marguerite remembers looking at her mother, and noting that she was impressed. There had been all this praise before and now mother and daughter were confronted by somebody who had taken Marguerite enormously to task. Was this someone who really knew what she was talking about? Or, was she one of those teachers who cruelly criticises merely to impress?

Marguerite's mother decided then that Gertrude Azulay should become the piano teacher of her two daughters.

Marguerite and Dolly were very frightened of Gertrude, and of what she thought of their playing. The two girls were sometimes filled with terror as they approached her door, and the lessons were to go on for many years!

Were the abrasive tactics of Gertrude Azulay justified?

Marguerite admits that a new road was opened up for her. She survived the Azulay onslaught, but does not now think it is a particularly good way of teaching. To have one's spirit crushed can be more damaging to a performer than to have slight defects in technique. Is it not fire, passion, feeling, in music which moves an audience? Wrong notes, faulty technique can be temporarily forgiven if the dynamics in the performance express the feeling of the music. Technique can be improved. That is the teacher's job. But a crushed spirit. . .?

Marguerite's recollection of these early lessons with Gertrude Azulay are very revealing.

'Gertrude always wore a hat when she was teaching, and the whole time there would be a cigarette in the side of her mouth, and when she said something, ash would drop all over the piano keys!'

There is little doubt that Gertrude grew to love her favourite pupil and it was not long before Marguerite was receiving letters which began, 'My darling M. . .'.

The good that Gertrude Azulay did for Marguerite was to teach her how to practise.

This was invaluable and Marguerite is very grateful for that. Gertrude Azulay taught her how to practise slowly, extremely slowly. Marguerite, under the guidance of her mother and then under Mr. Barron and Mr. Knott, had always 'used' her fingers, but Gertrude developed the pupil's fingers in a colossal fashion. Marguerite Wolff's hands are small. She is right-handed but believes that pianistically her left hand is stronger than her right. As a result of Azulay's teaching she has no difficulty in 'balancing' the hands while playing.

Gertrude Azulay taught Marguerite how to listen, and how to analyse . . . listening to every note, with the fingers coming down very slowly. In practising a scale there has to be complete equality, distance, and sound between each consecutive note.

The speed of playing the scale must begin very slowly, with the tempo increased gradually, ultimately obtaining what Gertrude referred to as the 'pearly touch'. The emphasis of the early lessons was in getting this 'touch'. The Spanish recognise the importance of touch by saying, 'toco el piano' (I touch the piano) rather than the English, 'I play the piano'. Gertrude then introduced a more mature 'touch' which she referred to as the 'held touch'. This 'touch' is especially necessary when playing big works, say, Brahms or Beethoven.

There were, of course, formal exercises by such teacher-composers as Schmitt, and Beethoven's pupil Czerny who opened up a new field of piano technique which is still valid today, along with such evergreens as the Bach 'Forty-eight' and the Chopin studies. Azulay taught in the following manner.

Practice of scales leads on to chordal work. Here there must be complete equality of sound, and the pupil must listen and make sure that the balance of the notes in the chord is absolutely right. Where should the emphasis be? The top, the middle, or the bass? Usually the emphasis is required at the top. It is essential to make sure that all the notes of the chord go down together, and to listen carefully one has to, first of all, play the chords slowly. It is thus easier to concentrate.

Naturally, it is bad only to practise slowly. The pupil needs to work up the tempo until it is as stipulated by the composer.

Sometimes young pupils play with one hand behind the other in tempo and that can best be corrected by playing slowly at first.

It is important to do right hand practice by itself, then left hand practice, and then, and this is absolutely essential, both hands must be put together then . . . not at some later hour. A pupil should not begin a difficult piece by practising both hands simultaneously. The hands should be worked separately and then played together. In performance it sounds very bad if one hand 'drags'.

19

It is also bad to anticipate an ornament. If the ornament is written *on* the beat then that is where it has to be played, and not before the beat. Should a composer want an ornament played on the bar then that is where he will write it. Much concentration is required to interpret correctly the composer's wishes in respect to ornaments.

Likewise, with the split chord. When the hand span is too small to accommodate all the notes of a chord, as in a lot of Schumann and Brahms, the chord has to be separated, quickly. Many pupils in this situation play the bottom note before the actual beat. The bottom note must be *on* the beat, and that is when the chord must be split.

All these things can be identified if the pupil learns to 'listen'. By this means one can gain control of the keyboard.

As pianists, we humans have been given by nature a very unequal hand, with a most odd shape. The fingers have different strengths so, to play evenly, the pianist has to make each finger as strong as the thumb.

Schmitt (and others) provide pages of exercises with sustained notes, and these are marvellous exercises for individual finger strength. The five fingers hold down five notes, and then one finger at a time is required to play with the other four still held down. Then two fingers, say, second and fourth with first, third and fifth held down. These exercises produce strong fingers and each with equal strength.

That was the basis of the technical aspect of Gertrude Azulay's piano teaching. All very orthodox, but she had the dominating personality which ensured that her pupils practised conscientiously and with full concentration.

The first two or three weeks were something of a battle of personalities between teacher and pupil. Marguerite appreciated the value of practice and the development of finger technique, but, all work and no play? . . . it was 'playing' the piano that Marguerite loved most. That was the driving force behind her self-imposed discipline. To quote Marguerite's own words, 'after about three weeks she somewhat grudgingly gave me what I wanted'. An actual piece of music to play!

The teaching was extraordinarily thorough, and Gertrude developed in herself a devoted interest in Marguerite's playing. Nothing was too much trouble, no explanation was left until the pupil had fully grasped its meaning . . . and always the teacher was thinking how best to further her pupil's career. For long periods there were lessons every day, and for many of these Gertrude would make no charge.

Marguerite and Dolly were attending a remarkable school called Kingsley. Nina and Walter had chosen the school for their daughters because it was rather continental in style. Most of the teachers were ex-Girton girls. There were four headmistresses and one of them was Professor Stebbing who had the chair in Philosophy, at Bedford College. The school covered the 'whole' curriculum but, because the school day began early, lessons ended at 2.00 p.m., an ideal time for a girl who wanted to hurry home and do her piano practice.

When Marguerite's piano lessons had been going on for a few years (she was then about thirteen) Gertrude took Marguerite along to Trinity College of Music, London, so that the Principal, Stanley Roper, could hear her play.

Stanley Roper was a very great man; aesthetic, charming, and organist of the Chapel Royal. He was very impressed with Marguerite's playing.

Sir Granville Bantock was also there. He was very old and Marguerite remembers that he looked like Brahms.

The two men conferred with other dignatories at Trinity College and then offered Marguerite a senior scholarship. Dolly was soon to follow Marguerite to Trinity College.

Gertrude Azulay was overjoyed that her faith in the young schoolgirls had been so generously confirmed.

Nevertheless, teenage Marguerite found it difficult to continue lessons at school, lessons with Azulay, and being a senior scholar at Trinity College of Music, all at the same time. Getting up at 6.00 a.m. and working extremely hard until bedtime was a discipline which has stood Marguerite well in later life. If there is anything to be learnt from her experience it is that such dedication, if kept balanced and sensible, brings with it the rewards of mental and physical health and a certain timeless youthfulness. Music, or any art, craft or creative occupation, can give the devotee this ageless vitality of youth. Pianists like Rubinstein and Benno Moiseiwitsch, Prime Ministers like Gladstone and Churchill, were 'young' in their seventies, and in three of them, their 'eighties' too, because the dedication to their work was of an ageless quality. If there is any formula for nigh-eternal youthful zest, then it must lie in the personal dedication to one's art, craft and general love of life. From this there is no 'retirement age'. There can be no finer gift for anyone than to find a purpose in life and follow it with disciplined concentration. Within that discipline there can be much fun. Dedication to one's purpose in life is not 'all work and no play'. Work and play should always be complementary, and Marguerite discovered this at an early age.

There are all sorts of rewards, not least the reward of being excited.

It was an exciting moment for schoolgirl Marguerite Wolff to be selected to play under Sir John Barbirolli. It was an exciting moment for Dolly to appear in a film with Mark Hamburg. (If we may depart from the Marguerite Wolff story very briefly we can enjoy an example of the humour musicians share by recording the often told Savage Club story of Mark Hamburg being chosen to play the part of Beethoven in a film. He rushed to tell his good friend and fellow-pianist, Benno Moiseiwitch, '. . . and I'm playing the part of Beethoven!' 'Ah, good!,' said Benno, 'and who's playing the piano?').

Gertrude Azulay was too big and powerful to be thought of as a Fairy Godmother, but she did surround Marguerite with these wonderful musical experiences; famous musicians, famous orchestras and conductors, and famous concert halls.

Marguerite and Dolly were at the tender age when much of it was taken for granted. They would be asked into the boardroom of Trinity College of Music for tea with the Doctors of Music, the Knights of music, the leading composers and conductors of the day. These eminent people would chat with the young sisters, and the two girls remember it now as a tremendous treat and something rather magical. Dr. Greenhouse-Allt became Principal of Trinity College of Music and he, too, was an enthusiastic supporter of Marguerite's career. (He was soon to appoint her the youngest teacher ever at the college).

Marguerite got her music exams, Licentiate and Fellowship, out of the way while she was still in her early teens. Officially she would not be able to use the Fellowship until she was twenty-one. It did not matter because by now she was playing professionally, and with leading orchestras.

Until this stage the decisions had been made by Marguerite's teachers and parents, and they had guided her career carefully and always with the best intentions in mind. There was never any of the exploitation into which gifted children are sometimes forced. She had been 'nursed along' very sensibly.

The first time Marguerite remembers actually wanting to have a say in a particular step in her career was when she was pleased to agree to enter for the Bambridge Scholarship, held once every three years.

By now Marguerite had realised that although she belonged to a happy family they were not enormously rich.

The four children had each been well educated, but Nina and Walter had to struggle to see that these various careers were financed. There was financial reward for the winner of the Bambridge but there was competition from many countries. The Bambridge Scholarship was worth £300 a year, a princely sum for a young girl to earn at that time.

The scholarship, named after its founder, was for three years and it was held triennially at Trinity College of Music in London. The chances of success seemed loaded against Marguerite; she already held a senior scholarship and had gained L.T.C.L. and F.T.C.L. status, so there was opposition to her entering.

Marguerite was determined to enter. Being a 'Bambridge' carried a lot of prestige, and one was expected to do much in return. It was the sort of success-with-responsibility that she wanted to win. Granville Bantock was one of the adjudicators and he well knew Marguerite's merit, having attended her concerts whenever he had been able to.

When Marguerite was declared the winner her joy was coupled with the happy feeling that at last she was contributing to her own future and taking some of the financial load off her parents.

It was as though her career had taken a major step forward.

The directors of Trinity College of Music are known to have said of the two young sisters, 'We're very proud of our Bambridge and our Baby!'

Among the older musicians who admired and advised Marguerite was the Hungarian cellist, Ludwig Lebell. He was a remarkable character who might greet you, 'Shake the hand that shook the hand of Brahms!' Ludwig had actually played the Brahms' cello/piano sonatas with the great composer at the piano. Marguerite was first-choice pianist with Ludwig Lebell's chamber music group at Trinity College of Music. She studied chamber music with Ludwig three times a week. The chamber music group included the talented violinist from Cyprus, Manoug Parikian.

Ludwig Lebell was keenly interested in Marguerite's career and he gave her some advice, but it was very different from the Azulay philosophy.

On the one hand there was solid Gertrude Azulay, proud of her pupil, and resolutely convinced that any deviation from the existing path would be utterly ruinous for Marguerite.

On the other hand there was the mercurial old cellist, Ludwig Lebell, whispering sacrilege in the young girl's ear.

'This Azulay, she's a very good woman, but forget your Scholarship. Give it up. Leave England. Go abroad. Go to Paris. If I had the money I'd send you there myself. Gertrude

23

Azulay is a good woman, but she's taken you as far as she can. Study with Cortot. Look what this has done for Solomon!'

Dolly remembers a typical Lebell incident. She was about 12 or 13, and was playing the piano with Ludwig's chamber music group. The Hungarian's English was not too brilliant, and he often started the music by counting, 'Eine, zwei, drei . . .' instead of 'one, two, three . . .'.

While Dolly was playing with the group Lebell began shouting at her, 'Like a sausage! Like a sausage!' . . . and Dolly didn't know whether he was referring to the music or to her, or whether it was German sausage or an English . . . in short, she began to panic, 'Like a sausage!' he repeated, his hands moving in a circle.

Fortunately the violinist understood Ludwig's outrageous use of the English language and he whispered to Dolly, 'He means "a rounded tone"!'

Marguerite does not remember the question of Paris being a big thing in her mind. She was still at the young age when life seems to solve problems with a fairly easy-going inevitability

Winning the Bambridge was probably the deciding factor in determining Marguerite's immediate future. Although she suspected that Ludwig Lebell was right, and now in retrospect she can see that he *was* right, it was also the right thing to do to respect loyalty. This included loyalty to her parents, who were proud of her success, and also to Trinity College who had treated her so fairly. It never seriously occurred to Marguerite that, having won the Bambridge, she should give it up. She does not remember there being any mental tussle. Rather was it a question of doing nothing precipitous. Marguerite and her family took a reasonably sophisticated view of life, but, for their daughter to drop everything and go to Paris, while still a teenage girl, it was obviously not the right thing to do.

It dawned on her parents and close friends that it was not really a question of Azulay versus Paris. In its simplest form, the problem was merely one that the time had come for a change. There were other ways of moving on from the tutelage of Gertrude. Indeed, it was not the piano teaching alone which caused Marguerite to rebel and Ludwig to advise a break.

Gertrude was preaching a philosophy, a way of life, quite alien to that which her family believed in and loved.

Gertrude Azulay, following her own life style, was trying to make Marguerite into a musical nun.

Two

'You can hear the dusters in her playing!' Gertrude Azulay snorted. She was referring to any girl pianist who dared to get married, but the barb was intended specifically for Marguerite.

Marguerite remained silent.

Here was the rift in the lute.

And such a boring rift because it was always on the same theme. There might have been a lighter touch, even a touch of humour, had Gertrude produced variations on the theme, such as, 'You can hear the nappies flapping on the clothes line!' or, 'You can hear the drone note of the Hoover!' But no. The theme remained infuriatingly 'sequendo'.

Teacher and pupil would never agree on the role women pianists should play in life, and Gertrude would never agree with Marguerite as to what was a 'full' life for a woman.

Perhaps Gertrude truly believed she was protecting her pupil.

Marguerite was an extremely attractive teenager. School friends of her two brothers had been in and out of the home for years, and were now discovering, that Marguerite and her sister made excellent partners for dances, parties and other social occasions. Marguerite had admirers, and these were, to Gertrude Azulay, 'the enemy'.

(Marguerite, however, found most young men rather boring. They had their way to make in life and were rather ego-centred. Men who were more mature, who had reached the top and were consequently more at ease with themselves, were attracted to Marguerite and her music, and it was with men of this calibre that Marguerite formed several important friendships).

Azulay was not a feminine woman. Marguerite never thought of her as anything else but a music teacher. Apart from her own world of music Gertrude's only other devotion seemed to be to an old aunt, referred to as 'Miss Bella'. Gertrude preached that one should only be in the world of music, with no distraction. She was trying to indoctrinate her pupil. She became almost desperate in her vocal attack on 'outside influences'. Marguerite could not accept the Azulay belief that a concert pianist must be above and removed from what Gertrude savagely referred to as 'Domestic Lust'.

This was too much for Marguerite. She was now at an age when she was beginning to appreciate the family relationship created by her parents, Nina and Walter. She closed her eyes and compared the grim picture of a concert pianist as presented by Gertrude Azulay with the warm and loving picture presented by her own family.

Marguerite very much appreciated the delightful world created by her parents, a world in which the children could enjoy life to the full and at the same time achieve success in their individual studies and life styles. All the resources at the disposal of her parents had gone into their four children.

Her father's face was a picture of divine happiness when he entered the Artists' Room after his daughter had given a concert. It was something Marguerite looked for. Something as important as the applause of the audience.

Her mother had developed an Artists' Room manner, a self-effacing but protective technique. There might be present the sort of person who would talk to the artist for ten minutes . . . about some other pianist, if given the opportunity to proceed! Nina would usher the bore to the tray of glasses of wine, Walter would smile understandingly, and Marguerite would be free to accept the true guests who wished to offer congratulations.

Nina

Nina and Walter were quite well-known as 'a couple'. Audiences looked out for them. On social occasions they were inevitably 'together' in more ways than the obvious, and at home they were always 'as one' with the children, any differences having been ironed out in the privacy of their own room.

Marriage, family, children; these were the very essence of Marguerite's idea of a 'full' life.

Just as when she was very young she had known that she would be a pianist, now that she was older she knew that one day she would have a 'home of her own', and it would be a tribute to her parents. She would care for her own children as her parents had done for theirs. The influence of Nina and Walter would be evident in many ways. They had impeccable taste. Nina was particularly aesthetic. She was, in a small way, a collector of beautiful things. One of her favourites was a collection of Bristol Blue glass.

Walter

Her favourite colours were blue, white, gold, and Marguerite knew that one day her own interior decorations and furnishing would reflect these gentle colours. There would be . . . what was Gertrude Azulay saying? Her words were now an intrusion upon Marguerite's dreams.

'Once a girl gets married you can hear the domestic dusters in her playing!'

'Repetizione, con forza!' thought Marguerite to herself.

Her agents at that time were using a 'glamour' picture of Marguerite, taken by a German photographer, Herr Schenker. It showed Marguerite in a strapless dress and it appeared not only on programmes and concert hand-outs but also on large posters. Gertrude Azulay; prude, puritan, female Svenghali, was not above hanging this glossy photograph on the wall above her piano. It served as a reminder to all her pupils, 'See what Azulay piano teaching can do!'

Even when Gertrude was a very old lady, Marguerite's picture remained in place on the wall.

And there were these letters, always beginning, 'My Darling M. . . .'

It was going to be very difficult for Marguerite to leave Gertrude. The teacher-pupil bond was very tightly locked, and Gertrude would not readily take part in any unlocking of that bond. Gertrude Azulay had an enormous possessive love in the teacher-pupil relationship she shared with Marguerite. Together they had progressed quite firmly in the world of professional piano playing. From Gertrude's point of view it was a relationship in which she, the teacher, was absolutely indispensible. She would be deeply offended, mortally insulted, if anyone suggested that the time had come for Marguerite to move on. At that time Marguerite did not have the nerve to discuss the matter with Gertrude Azulay.

Dolly also confirms that Azulay was utterly fanatical, believing that a musician should have no other interest but music. At concerts, when Azulay appeared, girl pupils would part from their boy friends.

'I turned up for a lesson and I was wearing a new coat and Gertrude Azulay said it was a poor thing that I could find time to go and buy it,' Dolly recounts.

Nina and Walter, and one or two of their close friends, could understand the problem facing Marguerite and it was the artist, Hillman, who came up with a splendid idea.

(Hillman's art work was principally in stained glass. He was married to a doctor, and his five sisters were all connected with the medical profession).

He reasoned that Marguerite was now past gaining much from piano lessons with Gertrude Azulay. She was a talented young concert pianist who had already played with London's leading orchestras and under famous conductors, including Sir John Barbirolli. What she really needed now was to work with a great master. Hillman was a personal friend of the famous pianist, Solomon. Solomon (the family name was Kutner) was born in London but had travelled the world extensively. He was clearly a first class choice to help Marguerite on her way to the top. A telephone call was made and Solomon agreed to meet the young pianist.

The great man was living in Notting Hill Gate, London, in rooms above a dairy in Church Street. He found this to be an admirable arrangement because he could practise as much as he wanted.

Solomon listened to what Hillman had to say and, after most charmingly putting Marguerite at her ease, he asked her to play something.

Marguerite placed a muff very carefully on a nearby table and when Solomon asked what she was doing so furtively she confessed that in the muff there was a tiny hot-water bottle. Solomon laughed but complimented Marguerite on her wisdom.

'Put your little Solomon down and let me hear you play.'

'Solomon' has remained the nickname for the diminutive hot-water bottle ever since, and Marguerite still uses the same bottle to keep her hands warm. It has become not only an object of utility (except, of course, in the tropics), but also something of a talisman. It is one of Marguerite's two pre-concert essentials, the other being a bag of barley sugar sweets.

When Marguerite finished playing, the master concert pianist, Solomon, said that he was tremendously impressed, adding that Marguerite had real talent, real quality in her playing, and that with the right work she would become a fine pianist.

Solomon said he would be prepared to take Marguerite, on certain conditions, the primary one being that she did not play in public for at least six months. Another condition was that she should be prepared to practise only scales and exercises (very slowly) for a considerable period.

He thought one should arise early in the morning because one was fresh (not everyone would agree). This would be no problem to Marguerite because she had been getting up at 6.00 a.m. for years. She had become used to practising for two hours before she went to school, and lately had been doing the same thing before going to Trinity College of Music, for the senior scholarship, and then for the 'Bambridge'. She was now also teaching at the college, thus becoming its youngest professor.

For a pianist of Marguerite's ability Solomon would give two lessons a week, sometimes these might be for two hours, but there would be great elasticity in the actual length of time which would be regulated by the content and the need of the particular lesson. During some lessons Solomon and Marguerite might spend the whole time talking about the deeper aspects of a particular piece of music. Solomon would expect Marguerite to practise at least eight hours a day. He mapped out a timetable; 6.00 a.m., rise and practise; 8.00 a.m., go for a walk; return and have breakfast; work through the morning, with a short break at 11.15 a.m. for tea or coffee; and so on throughout the day.

So far, this was quite acceptable to Marguerite. It seemed to be a mature extension of the Azulay method.

'For six months I want you to do nothing but scales and exercises, dead slow, then gradually quicker.'

Solomon then added that he would not want her to play in public during this initial six-month period. No doubt there was good reason and, musically speaking, good sense in this stipulation. However, Marguerite already had an impressive list of concert dates lined up. Would it be wise to cancel these? Indeed, would it be possible?

Solomon agreed that it would be unprofessional to cancel engagements which had already been confirmed.

Marguerite, with Hillman, hurried home and she was thrilled to tell her parents that Solomon was willing to accept her as a pupil.

However, there were some immediate concert engagements which she had to honour.

While giving a concert at a London music club Marguerite met a lady accompanist, affectionately known in the profession as 'Jo. E. Lee'. Jo was receiving plenty of work, some of it from the Imperial Concert Agency, founded in 1939 by Anne Trotman and Frederic Marland.

Jo. E. Lee's advice to Marguerite was to accept as many engagements as possible. Even small engagements were worth taking at the beginning of one's professional career. It was important to become known and one never knew what the acceptance of a concert engagement might lead to, or who might be present. Jo. E. Lee became a good friend of Marguerite's and recommended her to the Imperial Concert Agency who did, incidentally, already know of Marguerite Wolff.

The reports on Marguerite's performances and her professional reliability, did much to build up her reputation with the Imperial Concert Agency. Gladys Cook, one of the partners in the agency, went specially to hear Marguerite who, on this occasion, happened to be playing the Liszt *E flat Piano Concerto*. Gladys was very impressed with the performance and also with the elegant and professional stage technique. She recommended that the Imperial Concert Agency promote Marguerite to their list of 'leading artists' and also that they arrange a recital for their new star.

(It was fitting that Marguerite was playing music by Liszt when Gladys Cook heard her because the word 'recital' was first used, in 1840, to describe a programme of live music and this was given by Liszt himself, in London).

The directors of the agency were extremely kind to Marguerite and they next arranged a major concert for her in which she again played the Liszt *E flat Piano Concerto*. Marguerite recollects that this was a very big start. Unknown to her, Victor Hochhauser was in the audience and he was, as we shall presently see, to play a big part in the direction Marguerite's career was to take.

At about this time another gentleman was to play a part in directing the course of her career.

This was Freddie Hermann, a wonderful violinist, a Warsaw Prize winner, and a star pupil of Carl Flesch. Freddie seemed to be a young man with a glittering career ahead of him.

He was Polish, and had been engaged to play the César Franck violin/piano sonata with the very gifted pianist, Adella Katovska, also Polish, and who was the wife of violinist, Felix Van Dyll. The couple lived in Hampstead, London.

Freddie and Adella were being coached for their César Franck performance by Louis Kentner.

Freddie had suddenly become a regular visitor to Marguerite's home and he enthused about the coaching he was receiving from Kentner. His excitement was contagious — and so was Dolly's, as we shall see.

Of course, Louis Kentner was a name well-known to everyone, in and outside the music profession. Louis was born in Karwin, Silesia, in 1905.* He came to England in 1935. He was first married to Alona Karbos, the Hungarian pianist, but is now married to Griselda, sister to Yehudi Menuhin's wife, Diana. (William Walton's *Violin Sonata* is dedicated to the two sisters; 'to Diana and Griselda').

Marguerite was receiving concert engagements from the C.I.A. (Circle of International Artists) and these included one with Freddie Hermann, at a church in Hampstead. It was at short notice so Marguerite asked Dolly if she would come along and turn the pages. The programme included the César Franck *Violin/Piano Sonata*, and Dolly obligingly attended.

After the concert Freddie was particularly attentive towards the two sisters, once more enthusing about the help he was receiving from Louis Kentner, in particular for an important concert where Freddie was booked to play with Adella, a piano pupil of Kentner.

* According to Grove 5.

30

Marguerite was used to eminent gentlemen seeking her company and from time to time she received telephone calls from admirers inviting her to a party, or out to dinner.

The morning after the Hampstead concert the telephone rang and Marguerite heard Freddie's voice. It came, however, as something of a surprise, when Freddie asked if he could speak to Marguerite's schoolgirl sister, Dolly.

Dolly, of course, remembers the arrival of Freddie in her life very vividly. She was 14 at the time. Having been to countless concerts Dolly was quickly able to recognise real talent. When she heard Freddie Hermann play the violin it was the sheer beauty of his playing that enthralled her.

Some time later, however, Freddie *did* ring Marguerite.

'Darling, you must study with Kentner. There is only one person. I have never heard such coaching. Forget everything else!'

So Marguerite rang Louis Kentner and he agreed to hear her play.

After Marguerite had played to him, Louis Kentner said, 'you play with all the authority of an experienced concert artist but without the thousand and one things which go to make a concert pianist!'

Louis Kentner

Master and pupil immediately began discussing music and it was a most exhilarating experience for Marguerite.

'I remember walking right down King's Road, Chelsea, and through the park, I was so elated. I felt that a dirty window had been wiped clean so that I could look through. It was that exact feeling. Kentner had cleaned a pane of glass, and I could begin to see clearly . . . it was a revelation!'

There is a series of books 'Yehudi Menuhin Music Guides', and the one entitled *Piano* is by Louis Kentner. An understanding of his teaching methods can be gleaned from this book and, consequently, we can better understand Marguerite's excitement if we examine some of the ideas advanced by the great pianist.

In the introduction to the book Yehudi Menuhin writes; 'It is typical of this distinguished man and musician that he has given us neither arid "theory" nor an abstract "method", but rather the feeling of sharing in a train of thought and music . . .'

Kentner gives practical advice, not a 'method', and the following quotations illustrate his attitude:

'No teacher ought to force his pupil to become, even in his physical attitudes, a copy of his master, but allow him to follow his own instinct.'

'In matters of piano technique so much depends on imagination, temperament, and imponderable things of the mind . . .'

'Technique is the ability, gained by experience and practice, to bring the anatomy of the human body to bear on the instrument, and in so doing to achieve the best possible results with the least possible exertion.'

There were many 'methods' prevalent in the first half of the twentieth century, but when these were put into writing they frequently ended up as a book so complicated it became incomprehensible. Tobias Matthay had schools all over the United Kingdom which taught his 'method'. One unkind colleague said of Matthay's books, 'I hear your books have been translated into every language except English!'

A former pupil of Matthay, university graduate James Ching, M.A., B.Mus. (Oxon), became an opponent and produced the 'James Ching Method'.

Perhaps men like Matthay and Ching make a mistake when they think all knowledge can be put into words.

Sydney Harrison, the concert pianist, asserts 'the great difficulty in writing books on piano-playing lies in the fact that a pianist is an athlete who thinks non-verbally'.

Louis Kentner, commenting on part of the Matthay method succinctly writes, 'this may work for some pianists'.

The late Arthur Schnabel used to declare that it did not matter in the least how a pupil was taught: 'he would grow up and fashion his own technique, according to his own personality'.

To this Louis Kentner added, 'No doubt this is true. But what hard, stone-breaking work, how many false starts, what desperation can be saved the young person by the understanding teacher who knows his job, and who does, after all, nothing more than show the pupil his own way to himself!'

Of technique, Kentner sums up with, 'ultimately you should lose all consciousness of technique. Hard work and practice help you to reach this ideal, and then technique ceases to exist and Art takes over — Art which is concerned with the higher things of the mind and the soul, amongst which it ranges freely and easily'.

This, then, was the kind of master Marguerite had been looking for, and arrangements were made for her to begin studying with Louis Kentner.

The happy success of her meeting with him formed the background behind two very important concerts for Marguerite, one in London with the London Symphony Orchestra and, during the same week, her debut concert in Paris.

For Dolly, a year passed before she met Freddie Hermann again. She had not gone out with him after he telephoned her the first time, but she felt very flattered, and excited at this first real offer of 'a date'. It was at least a year later when Dolly was doing some broadcasts with a Russian orchestra, and she was introduced to them, that her name, Dorothy Wolff, brought forth this comment, 'Oh, you're the girl Freddie's madly in love with!' Freddie had been doing some work with Marguerite. At a Wigmore Hall concert, when Marguerite was playing the César Franck with him, Dolly went to the Artists' Room afterwards. She had been spellbound with his playing. He was surrounded by admiring females. Even though he was not handsome the girls adored him because of his great talent and his great charm and humour. He saw Dolly, threw his arms around her and said one word, 'Dolly!' Freddie had the capacity to make any woman feel that she's beautiful and attractive. Dolly fell in love with him. She was only 15, too young to think of marriage, but their friendship had that tacit understanding.

Meanwhile, Marguerite was preparing herself for the two important concerts.

From the very beginning of her career Marguerite has always paid great attention to what she has worn when performing on the concert platform.

'When I begin to don my dress I feel that I am preparing myself for the occasion . . . I begin to get the momentum!'

Hitherto Marguerite's mother had been the inspiration behind the dresses.

'We will contrive,' she would say, and one of Marguerite's relatives, Aunt Essie (Esther), who was an excellent needle-woman, would make the final concert dress.

Marguerite was keen to have something special to wear for her debut in Paris, and one of her pupils at Trinity College of Music, a high-born Iraqi girl, inadvertently supplied the means. Some months previously this young lady had invited Marguerite home to dinner at Cheyne Walk, Chelsea. The two became friends and through this Marguerite found herself in the company of the Royal House of Iraq, and this included a Mr. Kardré, Lord Chamberlain to the Iraqi Household, who was based in Paris.

Prince Zaid, Iraqi Ambassador in London, with members of the Iraqi Embassy became great supporters of Marguerite Wolff. (Eventually she was offered the post of organising a Conservatoire of Music in Iraq, but it was not possible for Marguerite to take on this work).

Marguerite wrote to Mr. Kardré in Paris and asked for a length of dress material, and presently a length of magnificent silver lamé arrived, a fabric of breath-taking beauty.

Marguerite says that, in those now far-off days, she 'had heard that Norman Hartnell was a very good dress designer'. The fact that he made clothes for the British Royal Family did not deter Marguerite. She and Dolly, who was still in her last year at school, looked up Norman Hartnell's address, tucked the material into a bag, and naively trotted along to the great couturier's establishment in Bruton Street.

The Hartnell staff were simply marvellous.

The chief designer, an imposing French lady, listened respect-fully while the two young girls explained what they wanted. There was a concert in London with the London Symphony Orchestra and, the same week, a debut recital in Paris, under the patronage of Lady Diana Cooper, wife of the British Ambassador to Paris.

By the time the explanations had been completed Marguerite confesses that the grand atmosphere of the establishment was beginning to excite her. The main thing which continued to put her mind at ease was the extreme politeness of the *vendeuse* and the rest of the Hartnell staff. They were behaving as though it was an everyday occurrence for two young sisters to wander in with a length of material and demand that a dress be made. Nevertheless, it was a shock for the two girls when live models began to parade and display the latest fashions so it was the *vendeuse* who chose the style, to save the tongue-tied little girls any embarrassment.

A dominating fitter then began measuring Marguerite who was, by now, far too intimidated to make any protest or essay any comment.

It is of great credit to the Norman Hartnell staff that the visit passed off successfully. They must have reasoned that it was no mean feat for a young girl to give a performance in London with The London Symphony Orchestra and then to give a second performance in Paris during the same week. So Marguerite, an innocent in the world of *haute couture,* was given the regal attention afforded to all Norman Hartnell's illustrious customers. No doubt the Norman Hartnell staff also realised that Marguerite would be seen in an English dress in Paris, the home ground of Dior, Pierre Cardin, Chanel, Révillon, Saint-Laurent, Patou and Laroche. She would also be seen with one of Europe's most beautiful and best-dressed women, Lady Diana Cooper. What a remarkable experience for one so young as Marguerite.

The delightful end to this Norman Hartnell story is that far from charging Marguerite's parents the usual fee for such a dress, the bill was for a mere £14.

Sir Norman Hartnell, K.C.V.O., 1901-1979. A member of Norman Hartnell Ltd. staff, Ann Price, writes, "We were very interested to read your story about Marguerite Wolff as it was a typical gesture of that great man, Sir Norman Hartnell. He would certainly have remembered the occasion — he had a wonderful memory and was always more than delighted to please his clients.

The dress was a winner at the L.S.O. concert in London. However, Marguerite Wolff has never followed fashion in her choice of concert dresses, preferring to select something which is 'right' for the occasion. She still has the Hartnell dress and it is a tribute to her disciplined eating habits and love of ballet dancing that her measurements have remained the same throughout her career.

It was something of a patriotic triumph for her to take a British-designed dress to Paris.

Marguerite travelled by 'Golden Arrow' train (all her subsequent trips to France have been by air) and she stayed at a suite, lent to her by the Iraqi Embassy, at the Hotel Bristol, the luxury hotel in rue du Faubourg Saint-Honoré, the same street which still houses the British Embassy. Marguerite was driven to the British Embassy in the official Iraqi Embassy car and also to the Zionist Headquarters in Paris, thus proving that music can cut across political barriers despite the unrest in the Middle East at that time.

'This huge car would wait for me outside the hotel, and it drove me everywhere I wanted to go. I felt like the biblical Queen Esther!'

Had Marguerite been a reincarnation of the high-spirited joyous Esther she might well, on finding herself surrounded by the crazy traffic of Paris, have exclaimed Esther's gallant final words, 'If I perish, I perish!'

Marguerite very clearly remembers being greeted in the Artists' Room of Salle Pleyel by Lady Diana Cooper, wife of the Ambassador to France, the pre-war Cabinet Minister Duff Cooper (who later became Viscount Norwich).

'She was absolutely gorgeous and to my young eyes she was the epitome of feminine grace. I can still see this glamorous creature coming towards me, wearing an osprey hat, and followed by her attentive entourage!'

(It would seem that this 'absolutely gorgeous' lady has lost none of her vivacity because in May 1984, a British national daily newspaper described her as a 'Black-eyed beauty'. Lady Diana, 91 years young had an accident in the night. Speaking of her black eye she is reported as saying. 'I'm delighted with it — it's so perfectly big and round. I was staying in Paris with four friends and wandering in the dark from my room to the bathroom and I tripped on a step, and a hard piece of marble mantelpiece hit me in the eye!' It was the first time Lady Diana had visited France since she left in 1960. This remarkable widow had lost none of her former Ambassadorial wit or power of cryptic comment, 'I saw all my old friends but I didn't recognise them. They had all turned bald!').

This, then, was the lady who was patron for Marguerite's first trip to Europe's busy centre of music, Paris.

Marguerite received an excellent Press for her performance in London and in Paris, and she felt that the influence of Louis Kentner had been a major reason for her triumph.

The standard of her performance can be gauged from the reports of the critics, Claude Galtat being a typical example:

'A considerable choice of works of different styles and character gives evidence not only of the vast repertoire of Miss Wolff, but also of the great technical qualities of this pianist. In modern pieces, too, she showed herself above all a subtle musician, artistic, clothed in fine sonority, in charm and elegance.'

Claude Galtat, 'Paris Journal'

LA PIANISTE ANGLAISE
MARGUERITE WOLFF

donnera son unique Récital de la saison le 28 mai à la salle Chopin. La Cantatrice **Beatrice DELVA** prêtera son concours à ce concert.

(Dandelot.)

In this concert Marguerite played Chopin, Liszt and Schumann, and in the second half an interesting group of pieces; Spanish, French, and English.

She began with *Triana,* (Iberia Suite II) by Albeniz, who played the piano in public at the age of four and who became leader of the Nationalistic School of Spanish Composers. (He studied with Liszt at Weimar and Rome).

Next came the *Feux d'artifice* (Fireworks), by Debussy. The piece is the last of his *Preludes,* and the close finger patterns, with sudden leaps up and down the keyboard, rapid compound trills with hands interlocking, and brilliant cadenzas reminiscent of Liszt, make it an ideal showpiece for any concert pianist. It is a real box of pianistic virtuosity as explosive as any actual box of French fireworks.

The third piece in Marguerite's group was William Lovelock's *Concert Etude in C sharp minor,* a work specially written for her by the English composer.

Lovelock (writer of a 'students' bible' on harmony) had been one of Marguerite's professors at Trinity College of Music, and he had not only composed works for her but had arranged the Johann Strauss Waltz, *A Thousand and One Nights,* for her. This became a very popular item in her repertoire. She loved playing Lovelock's music and she remains a tremendous admirer of his work.

He went to Brisbane Conservatoire of Music and settled in Australia, in later years adding the role of music critic to his work as composer and arranger.

Marguerite's choice of music and her performance had been perfect and the Paris audience called for more.

After a really successful concert the artist often experiences a kind of intoxicated relief, a light-headed euphoria, a post-concert elation. It is not unknown in these circumstances for the artist to feel fresher than the organisers or, perhaps, even the audience, when the concert is over. The artist feels a need to celebrate, like the sports victor wearing the laurel and laughing as the victory champagne flows.

In such a mood as this Marguerite was taken to *La Mère Caterine* restaurant, in Montmartre and, like Chopin, Liszt, Berlioz (who, incidentally preferred his roistering to be accompanied by a guitar), Debussy, Offenbach, Satie, and hundreds of lesser-known artists. Marguerite played the wooden upright piano, wedged against the wall and hemmed in with tables, chairs, waiters, and eager-eyed diners. This was Montmartre — this was the special place on the hill which considered itself above and apart from the Paris below — and this is where Marguerite gave an impromptu performance — and what did she play? — *Fantasie Impromptu* — what else! — and the historic Gods who had made the *Chat Noir, Lapin Agile,* and the whole of Montmartre and Clichy vibrate to music in the past nodded their approval.

The next day Marguerite gave a concert at The British Embassy, and the Ambassador, his wife, and many other notables in the Diplomatic Service were present, including the Duke and Duchess of Windsor, and the Archbishop of Paris, in his red robes. The international flavour of her programme was particularly appreciated. Paris is the one city in the world which has retained its own distinct taste in music (the accordion being an essential ingredient) while also being the most international of music centres anywhere on earth.

Marguerite and her Montmartre chaperone, Nigel Pumphries, accepted an invitation to visit the studio of Raymond Duncan, brother of the notorious pre-war dancer, Isadora, who had strangled herself in Nice, in 1927, when her crêpe Chinese red scarf got entangled in the wheel of her moving Bugatti car.

Many people of the period judged Isadora to be simply a sensationalist, both politically and in her Grecian dancing (partly based on the callisthenics system of François Delsarte). Was she not an avid supporter of Russian Communism? Did she not dance practically naked? Was she not an atheist? Take away the sensational and was she left as a great artist? Her followers said, 'Yes!', her detractors, 'No!'

The naval attaché, Nigel, was knowledgeable on the Isadora affair and he was able to persuade Marguerite that the famous dancer was, despite all, very human and very much a great artist.

'Yes,' Nigel explained, 'Isadora did love Russia, but her major activity was the founding of a school of dancing for young

With Nigel Pumphries, La Mère Caterine, Montmartre, Paris.

Russian girls who showed talent. And yes, the barefooted
Isadora did appear in flimsy and scanty clothing, but her excuse
for exposing her limbs also exposed a delightful sense of humour.
In 1898, at the start of her career, there was a disastrous fire at
the Hotel Windsor, in New York, and all her costumes were
destroyed. So, she "improvised", (or, as Marguerite's mother
might have said, "she contrived"), with diaphanous Liberty silk
and a few colourful streamers.'

Marguerite listened attentively as she was being driven to
Raymond Duncan's studio.

'The American evangelist, Billy Sunday, poured scorn and
Hell-fire on Isadora — "that Bolshevik hussy who doesn't
wear enough clothes to pad a crutch". One can imagine her
unconcerned reply, "but my clothes were all burnt in the hotel
fire!".'

History records that Isadora became the pet of society, and
shocked but titillated audiences flocked to see the 'nude dancer'
(mayor of Indianapolis' description) in Budapest, Berlin, Paris,
Vienna and other European cities.

In 1923 the Paris *Tribune* had been kinder to Isadora and her
brother Raymond than the American Press. The French newspaper reported that 'the famous aesthetic dancer was draped in
a flowing robe of royal purple trimmed with gold', and of her
brother they stated, 'Raymond Duncan, who goes about Paris
barefooted and in Greek robes.'

Isadora danced at the Théâtre Raymond Duncan, in Paris,
and between 1923 and her death in 1927 she and her brother
lived alternately at rue de la Pompe in Paris and 343 Promenade
des Anglais in Nice.

Raymond's post-war studio was, however, near the Palais
Royale. During the Second World War he harboured more than
two hundred refugees in his studio, under the very noses of the
Nazi conquerors of Paris.

This was the man Marguerite was being taken to meet.

'Your name, even the spelling, will interest him,' Marguerite
was told, 'because for Isadora's last concert, at the Mogador
Théâtre, where she danced Schubert's *Ave Maria,* and Wagner's
Death of Isolde, the orchestra was conducted by an Alber
Wolff!'

Although the war had been over for some time, tales of
Resistance bravery were still very much in vogue. Isadora's
brevity of costume had been equalled by Josephine Baker when
she took Paris by storm 'wearing only a blue and red ring of
feathers around her hips', as she danced. This sense of daring
had been evident, in a different way, during the Nazi occupation

of Paris, when Josephine engaged in dangerous clandestine activities for the Resistance. The Gestapo discovered this, and Josephine was invited to dine with Field Marshall Goering. She had been forewarned that the fish was poisoned (cyanide). After being forced to eat it, at gunpoint because she at first refused, she was allowed to go to the Ladies Room. Instead, she jumped into the laundry chute at the bottom of which she was quietly caught by waiting Resistance workers, rushed to a secret hospital, and her life was saved by the speedy use of a stomach pump. She was awarded the Croix de Guerre, and the Rosette of the Legion of Honour.

Raymond Duncan was of this wartime heroic stock.

It was with a certain suppressed excitement that Marguerite entered the crowded studio.

There were poets, dancers, artists, musicians, and many journalists, and there was also an expectancy in the air. Sunday afternoons at the Raymond Duncan studio were special. 'Everybody' wanted to be there, to be seen there. For many it was the hallmark of social and artistic success.

Then Marguerite saw Raymond.

She remembers clearly his spindly legs under his Roman toga. He wore sandals, and was very pale, quite old, but alive and alert. He was a small man. Marguerite was not particularly impressed.

In one corner of the studio there was a small stage on which stood a baby grand piano. Many journalists seemed to be wandering in. As Marguerite composed herself the faces gradually turned, one by one towards the stage, the conversations petered out, and when all eyes were on Mecca, Raymond led Marguerite towards the piano, and she played for the assembled guests.

In retrospect, the official recital at Salle Pleyel, the radio broadcasts, the nocturnal visit to Montmartre, the Sunday afternoon Chopin impromptus at Raymond Duncan's studio, the glittering soirées at The British Embassy, the magnificent suite at the Hotel Bristol, the Embassy car, and the enthusiastic invitations to return to Paris, made Marguerite's first visit to the French capital all she had dared to hope for from this magical city.

There were to be four visits during Lady Diana Cooper's reign as hostess at The British Embassy. Each subsequent visit was magic, but the first . . . that was the most exciting! There is nothing more memorable than a first time. No wonder Ludwig Lebell had urged her to go to Paris!

Marguerite returned to London and in the way that changes

are made in one's life, she found herself busy with a timetable of teaching at Trinity College, giving concerts and lecture-recitals, and . . . the new aspect of her career . . . studying with Louis Kentner.

After Paris, life seemed placid enough but it was, in addition, a period of great development for Marguerite. She found that Kentner did not choose music for her to study. Instead, he worked on the music she took to him and this was, usually, music she was studying for her concert repertoire. One day Kentner said to Marguerite, 'I hear you have a very talented sister.'

Dolly had left Gertrude Azulay and had been without a teacher for some time. She went to Louis Kentner's studio and he agreed to take her on. The first lesson was a tremendous success. Dolly comments now that it was as if he had said, 'Look at these Golden Gates, I'm going to open them for you!' Dolly believes that whatever Kentner had done he would have been brilliant because he has a first class brain. 'I think he's one of the greatest musicians in the world.'

When Dolly turned sixteen her friendship with Freddie Hermann was gladly accepted by her family, but they were worried about his health. He was not looking very well at all.

Dolly herself takes up the story.

'He was touring with the Anglo-Polish ballet and one day he complained of a stiff neck. I suggested that he had probably been in a draught during all the touring. I had known him less than two years but I was gloriously happy with the relationship. He was a natural womaniser. If we had married I would have been tremendously happy for a time, but at my age marriage was something for the distant future. He decided to see the doctor on Monday, who immediately sent him to Middlesex Hospital. He had leukemia. I visited the hospital. I remember taking a poster of a concert I was giving in Queen Mary Hall. Freddie was whiter than white, despite several transfusions. I said, "I *know* you're going to get better." He had just bought a piano so that we could start our piano/violin musical life together. Freddie smiled at me. He said, "My head is so bad, do you think you could get a flannel and put it in cold water." I remember going to the wash basin, I was totally undomesticated, I had never made a cup of tea or boiled an egg, because my mother always said any intelligent woman could learn all that any time. I was lacking in common sense, and little things got out of proportion. I was desperately wanting to do the right thing; should I wring the flannel out? — When I gave the concert, I played for Freddie. I thought, "Freddie, you *are* at the concert. I'm playing for you!" Even today people remember that concert because I played my best. I said, "I *know* Freddie's going to be all right. You *must*!" I thought my strength would make him better. At that age you think you can move mountains, and then you find you can't. Two days later Freddie died. I had an utter feeling of desolation, and I felt, what can I do with my life without Freddie? My life is finished, I'll never be happy again. Of course, one does, you know.'

His death merited a long obituary in *The Times*. Music had lost a very promising artist.

It had been Freddie's infectious enthusiasm for the coaching of Louis Kentner which had directed Marguerite in that direction.

Meanwhile a second man was having a direct influence on Marguerite's career, and this was Victor Hochhauser. He had wandered into her concert with the London Symphony Orchestra when she was playing the Liszt *E flat Concerto*. He told Lynford and Joel, the young impresarios who were just starting their promotions business, that they would be wise to contact an up-and-coming pianist, Marguerite Wolff. Unknown to Marguerite, John Joel went to hear her play. Dolly remembers seeing this intent young man. Speed was essential because Marguerite had already been approached to share a world tour with the famous American singer, Paul Robeson.

One morning, Geoffrey Farmer, secretary at Trinity College of Music, took a telephone call. It was for Marguerite, so he sent for her.

The enquirer invited her to an office at 17 Cavendish Square. There was something urgent about the caller, a certain sincerity, but when he told her he was of the firm 'Lynford and Joel' it meant nothing to her. She had never heard of them. Could she come round in her lunch time? Marguerite found herself agreeing to do this.

'Who was that?' Geoffrey Farmer asked.

'Someone called John Joel.'

'Never heard of him!'

'Neither have I!'

Three

The concert at the Royal Albert Hall was a sell-out. It seemed very doubtful if those at the rear of the long queues would find standing room even in the top tier of the famous Victorian Hall in Kensington Gore. Undaunted by the mathematics of the situation the queues still inched their optimistic way forward, eager-eyed in the general exhilaration, the people holding tickets smiling confidently, individuals without tickets staring with calculating glances at the distant doorways set in the circular shape of the building.

Marguerite Wolff arrived at the Artists' Room which she was sharing with fellow artist, Tito Gobbi.

This great Italian singer had not appeared in England before but he had a vast British following because of his marvellous films, in particular, *The Barber of Seville*, made by an Italian film company and distributed throughout the Western world. His most famous roles were in *Tosca* (as Scarpia), *Rigoletto*, . . . both these operas had been filmed and shown in England, *Gianni Schicci, Falstaff,* Alan Berg's *Wozzeck*, and *Don Giovanni.* Tito was extremely handsome and he was billed as 'Italy's Most Romantic Singer.'

On the hand-out posters Marguerite's picture was the same size as Tito's.

The Albert Hall rehearsal had begun at 2 o'clock in the afternoon and most of the time had been taken up with the Italian baritone being accompanied by the Royal Philharmonic Orchestra, leader Oscar Lampe, and conducted by Muir Mathieson.

Tito's programme was Largo al Factotum (*The Barber of Seville,* Rossini), 'Prologne' (*I Pagliacci,* Leoncavallo) and 'Di Provenza' (*La Traviata,* Verdi).

It was a triumph for the two-year old business partnership 'Lynford-Joel Promotions Ltd.' to bring 'Italy's Most Romantic Singer' to London. The two impresarios had hired a Rolls-Royce to meet Tito at the airport.

Their other triumph of the evening was to pair Marguerite with Tito.

In his book, *I Paid the Piper,* John Joel writes, 'Cyril Smith, Iso Ellinson, and Phyllis Sellick were at the top of the profession, and were controlled by Ibbs and Tillett. When great names like Schnabel, Heifitz and Horrowitz came to England they belonged to Harold Holt. As impresarios we felt that our function was to build new starts. We had met Miss Wolff and we thought she was a most attractive personality who might well become a leading pianist in the mould of Eileen Joyce, whose success owed much to her own glamour. We expected to spend a lot of money on publicity for such a prospective star.'

Marguerite remembers well her initial visit to the Lynford and Joel offices at 17 Cavendish Square.

She had hurried there one lunchtime during her teaching duties at Trinity College of Music, in nearby Mandeville Place.

Mark Lynford and John Joel had formed their Promotion enterprise after World War Two and one of the first things they did was to try and bring the seventy musicians of the Palestine Symphony Orchestra to Britain, but the complicated travel arrangements broke down. They next tried the Hallé Orchestra under Barbirolli, Manchester being a little nearer to London than Tel Aviv. This was a successful venture and Lynford and Joel actually made £300 profit on the first concert.

For London concerts they principally used the Royal Albert Hall (7,000 with 1,000 standing), Central Hall (3,000), and Wigmore Hall (lucky to sell 500 tickets!) for soloists, including in their lists the following artists; Walter Midgeley, Olive Groves, Campoli, Leslie Bridgewater Quintet, Billy Mayerl. . . . These London concerts were not terribly successful. They were too much like Lyon's Corner House music, so, to quote from John Joel's book, 'Marguerite Wolff was the bright new prospect.'

Marguerite recollects, 'They asked me if I'd like to play in South Africa and, if so, could my mother or an aunt accompany me. I spoke to my family afterwards. My mother could not travel to South Africa, but I did have an aunt living there. Her husband had been in the Boer War. I also had a London aunt, Eva, who was very excited when I mentioned South Africa to her because her daughter, Violet, had been born there. Violet Goodman now lives in Eastbourne and is a wonderful specialist pianist for ballet music. So, things looked bright for the South African adventure. However, it did not come off. The first thing Lynford and Joel did for me was to arrange a very successful concert at the Wigmore Hall, for which they paid me an excellent fee.'

(It was not unknown in those days for a novice *to pay* £150 for the privilege of playing at Wigmore Hall. Few artists expected to make much of a profit there. Why did they do it? Because there was the hope of a good report from the music critics and this could be used to promote further concerts and attract the interest of leading agents).

John Joel.

44

Beginning with the comparatively highly-paid Wigmore Hall concert Marguerite Wolff became Lynford and Joel's star piano performer.

And here she was now, hurrying for her big night, sharing equal billing with the great Italian star, Tito Gobbi.

The Artists' Room was filled with cigarette smoke. (Marguerite is a non-smoker). Tito Gobbi had been, and was still, chain-smoking when Marguerite arrived. She claims that she is nervous before a concert, but Tito Gobbi! . . . he seemed to be infinitely worse. It appeared that he had struck up a close friendship with John Joel who was fussing around the Italian singer, soothing him, encouraging him, and seeing to his every need. It soon became apparent that his 'every need' included a new shirt. The one he was wearing was saturated with perspiration.

John Joel sent out for a new white shirt.

Marguerite recalls that despite Tito's obvious nervousness he 'seemed very sophisticated, not very typical of being an opera star, but enormously charming'.

The veneer of sophistication and the delightful evidence of charm were attributes enhanced by the presence of Tito's wife, Tilde, who was with him on this first visit to London.

Tito Gobbi was born in Bassano del Grappa in the Veneto. He went to Rome to study and there he met Tilde, daughter of one of Italy's foremost musicologists. He married Tilde and she had an aristocratic poise and assured manner which was very much to the advantage of Tito Gobbi.

Marguerite reflects on her meeting with Tilde at The Albert Hall, and their subsequent friendship, 'She was rather restrained, extremely aristocratic, cultivated, patrician, quite magnificent for a big star. She was not beautiful. She was not possessive, she let Tito have all his glory, there was enormous strength in her, this complete culture. She was a wonderful hostess, she was magnificent, she never obtruded. Tito was always the star, but she must have stabilised him tremendously, and she never tried taking the floor. She was just perfect for him, in his position. Although she was a high-born Italian she was extremely nice, rather gentle, but she could make some very pertinent remarks. Her observations were very acute. I imagine she managed the business side of his life very well.'

Tilde was also an excellent pianist and frequently accompanied her husband in song recitals. She was his accompanist at The Palace Theatre, Shaftsbury Avenue, at a charity concert.

(Charity concerts were free of Entertainment Tax. Some impresarios set up tax-free societies to promote concerts in aid of charities. The profit went to a charity instead of in tax).

Tilde, despite her upper class background and familiarity with big occasions, was struck by the atmosphere and headiness pervading the smoke-filled room tucked away in the bowels of the enormous Albert Hall. Of the concert hall itself she later wrote, 'My, what a hall. We were terrified by its immensity!'

The concert began with the Royal Philharmonic Orchestra playing Beethoven's *Leonora Overture No. 3*. Then Marguerite played the Beethoven *Piano Concerto No. 3 in C Minor*.

It was not only important for Marguerite herself that her performance be excellent, but also for the future of Lynford and Joel Promotions Ltd., and also for Tito Gobbi's 'first appearance' that night. The audience must be won over at the start of the evening. Marguerite needed to be at her brilliant best to set the audience in the right mood to receive the highly nervous Italian baritone. The British knew of him only through his films and records. How would they react to him 'in person'. There was also one other fear for the promoters; how would the British react to an Italian so soon after the war?

Music, probably more than any other art or culture, can raise people of all creeds and nationalities to a common level. It was tactful to put the British artist on first. Such nationalistic titles as 'British' and 'Italian' would be forgotten, and the common denominator 'Artist' would apply. It only required Marguerite's performance to be sublime . . . and the rest of the concert would then have the setting for total triumph.

The concert *was* a triumph.

After Tito's arias, the orchestra brought the concert to a close by playing Beethoven's *Symphony No. 5*.

Then there was a standing ovation for the two artists, and for Muir Mathieson and the Royal Philharmonic Orchestra.

Lynford and Joel acted quickly and announced from the platform that Marguerite and Tito would give a second concert. (Provisional arrangements had been made with the Albert Hall). There was a stampede at the box office.

And in the Artists' Room?

'There was a moment when Louis Kentner came in, he put his arms out and embraced me, I was very moved, it was an emotional moment, I still curtsey to him when he comes in the Artists' Room, like the ballerina to the ballet master.'

Tilde wrote, 'The concert was a fantastic success . . . so many people in the dressing room, we thought we were going to be suffocated out, we were positively assaulted and were afraid we would be torn to pieces.'

And Marguerite remembers, 'The concert still remains in my memory, as clear today as then. After the concert it was so

Picture taken during 'Lynford and Joel' era.

exciting to be in the Artists' Room. There were so many people there, it was full of love and happiness, my parents and family, so many saying, "to think that I held her on my knee". Despite all the professional playing I had done, the Albert Hall concert with Tito was really a major step forward in my career. You're suddenly emerging, you've arrived at a certain point in your musical life. After that it's the same, but not the same. I haven't had a lot of acrimony in my life, but you do begin to get a little bit of the green eye, but at the Tito Gobbi night, the Artists' Room was full of love, the agents were thrilled, there was a huge Gobbi following. Lynford and Joel took us to a big party at the Hungaria Restaurant. I was sitting next to Louis Kentner. Joseph Vecchi, who ran the restaurant, unlocked the piano, and Gobbi was asked to sing, and then I was asked to play, and it was all very exciting. Vecchi would send more champagne to our table. There were about twenty of us. But, when I eventually got home, my mother and father always left me a little note, with their own personal feelings, and such was the reaction after the concert that I went to bed and cried myself to sleep. One can get very depressed after a concert. People talk of post-pregnancy depression . . . a big let-down . . . no reason, it's just reaction.'

As it turned out, however, the ones who could justifiably 'cry themselves to sleep' were Lynford and Joel.

Following the success of the Albert Hall concert they understandably expected Tito Gobbi to be in demand all over the country, on radio, and at places like Covent Garden Opera House. To the bewildered dismay of Mark Lynford and John Joel, none of these things happened, at least, not immediately. A number of minor factors added up to create a major problem.

For example, there was a strong Italian following in London, but not so much elsewhere in the country. There was also newspaper rationing so there was no space for the sort of 'gossip' that Tito Gobbi's arrival would have merited in easier times. Once the main news items, football results, strikes, and rationing information had been written there was no space left except to report that such-and-such a concert had taken place.

Advertising was a problem. Lynford and Joel went to great expense to have posters displayed, but in all towns and cities there were 'poster gangsters', that is, people who pasted their own posters over the professional ones. This became so bad that eventually Town and Planning Regulations outlawed this flyposting scandal. This much-needed legislation came too late to help Lynford and Joel during the first British tour of Tito Gobbi.

(To give just one example; the previous year Lynford and Joel had paid a local agent ten per cent of the face value of the tickets for a concert in Brighton if he would display large posters all over the seaside resort. When the intrepid impresarios visited Brighton there was no sign of even a single poster anywhere. All Lynford and Joel got from the Brighton agent was, . . . 'You know what it is . . . you pay to have them put up tonight, and tomorrow somebody over-posts them, and there you are!').

Reports of the Albert Hall concert were, surprisingly to Lynford and Joel, extremely cold and faint-hearted. There was a marked resistance to Tito Gobbi by the critics. Even more hurtful was a reply from the B.B.C. to Lynford and Joel's overtures on Tito's behalf because the B.B.C. Music Department suggested that 'he was past it' as far as radio work was concerned. (Tito was 35 and in his prime!). Covent Garden, too, showed no interest at first. They only wanted stars who could sing in English. It may have been Tito Gobbi's disadvantage that the Royal Opera House, Covent Garden, had already used an Italian baritone, Paolo Silveri, a 33 year-old six foot photogenic Italian who had already earned his popularity in England the hard way . . . by singing. A notable incident in Paolo's career had been in 1947 when, at a Yorkshire Evening Post sponsored Lynford and Joel concert (Marguerite also played in these concerts) at Leeds Town Hall, Paolo had been programmed to sing immediately after the Northern Philharmonic Orchestra, under Clarence Raybould, had played Beethoven's *Symphony No. 5,* the famous 'V' symphony, and Elgar's *Pomp and Circumstance March,* the 'Land of Hope and Glory' piece. Paolo Silveri, symbol of a defeated Italy, understandably threw a tantrum and refused to sing. To cut a long discussion short it is only necessary to record that eventually John Joel persuaded Paolo to go out and show the British what he was made of.

When Paolo's glorious baritone voice filled the hall with the Prologue from *I Pagliacci* (Leoncavallo), his singing and his sheer physical attraction overcame the lingering memory of 'Land of Hope and Glory', and Paolo was accepted! He also became a favourite singer at Covent Garden.

Lynford and Joel had great success with the Paolo Silveri concerts around the country, several of the concerts being shared with Marguerite Wolff.

Perhaps there was a psychological reaction by the conservative British. One Italian baritone had been accepted . . . but . . . you can have too much of a good thing! This attitude, outside London, might be termed as a typically British reaction at that time.

SILVERI ARRIVES—SINGING

COCKTAILS FOR TWO —
Marguerite Wolff and
Paolo Silveri at a reception
in Leeds last night.

Silveri had been with the San Carlo Opera Company, and when he arrived in England he could hardly speak any English. However, with that special facility Europeans have (and most English people do not have) Paolo soon learnt the language . . . and to good publicity effect . . . 'Your B.B.C. says my voice is not silver, it is gold!' It was not long after his arrival in London that he became the darling of Covent Garden, and 'society women chased him down the street'. Paolo's *Rigoletto* was unforgettable.

Marguerite Wolff, reflecting on the early days when she worked with Paolo, says, 'Paolo Silveri was one of the most marvellous artists, and he was also generous. Most artists would disappear when not actually performing, but Paolo would stand in the wings while I played my part of the programme, and he would listen, and shout "Bravo!" We became great friends and still are today.'

Lynford and Joel decided to go carefully over the expenses for the return Gobbi/Wolff concert at the Albert Hall.

The Musicians Union was at its most active, and was a little belligerent too. Like all unions, they were benefitting from an anti-establishment attitude by the British workers, and artists, following World War Two, when millions of men and women had been under military discipline. Now that the British had actually *won* the war they were not in any mood to be pushed around by bosses or management. Unions became very popular and union leaders ever more powerful. 'The Right to Strike' had been a hard-won concession and going on strike ('One Out! All Out!') had become a sort of Industrial Game, a wonderful excuse to 'cock a snook' at the boss. The inevitable demand for industrial peace was . . . more money!

In music, fees were set for the various grades of orchestral players. While on the one hand this made orchestras very expensive (and had a lot to do with the demise of the Big Bands) at least people like Lynford and Joel knew exactly how much a symphony orchestra would cost.

Tito Gobbi was going through a rough time during his first tour of Britain. The fame his films had brought him was counter-productive to his acceptance by the public as a live artist. Tito was at his best when he had an attractive soprano to play opposite to him. In his film *Tosca* the beautiful actress, Nelly Corredi, played the part of the heroine, but the singing voice was dubbed by a professional singer. The sound in all films was, anyway, dubbed after the actual shooting so the audience, knowing that Nelly wasn't doing the actual singing, also had doubts about Tito Gobbi. Was he just a film star?

50

In his professional life as an opera singer Tito was slightingly referred to as a 'film star' by some of his fellow opera-singers.

For the second Albert Hall concert Lynford and Joel did not bill Tito as 'Italy's Most Romantic Singer', but as, 'World Famous Italian Opera and *Film Star*' (italics mine). As it turned out 'Film Star' was not the best description to have chosen in the existing climate . . . but that is a judgement made now with the value of hindsight. At the time no one could have seen that the films which made him famous in Britain were counter-productive when it came to presenting him as a concert artist. It is, also, probably true that Tito Gobbi did not enjoy concerts half as much as singing and acting in opera. Who will ever forget his partnership with Maria Callas in *Tosca*! The two had their quarrels, 'nervous explosions' as Tito called them, but the two were always 'Tosca and Scarpia' . . . that was the sheer magic and electrifying brilliance of the great Tito Gobbi.

Trinity College of Music, who had such faith in Marguerite Wolff, boasted another star, Amy Shuard, the operatic soprano. Amy's early success was gained in a tour of South Africa and her most famous role was in Verdi's *Aida*. Amy sang with Tito Gobbi in the London production of Verdi's *Macbeth*.

The beautiful Elisabeth Schwarzkopf (second wife of the afore-mentioned Walter Legge) was yet another famous singer who paired with Tito. These two were especially marvellous in *Traviata*. Anna Magnani and Gina Lollobrigida also partnered Tito.

This, then, was 'his scene', . . . the operatic stage, whether in opera house or film studio, and singing with, and to, a beautiful soprano or actress.

Tito was not completely happy on a concert platform in 'a stuffed shirt' . . . albeit one John Joel had sent out for immediately prior to the Italian star's arrival on stage!

All in all, it was a wise decision by Lynford and Joel to employ, not an orchestra, but an accompanist for the second Wolff/Gobbi concert. They engaged Ivor Newton, second only to Gerald Moore as accompanist in London. Marguerite was quite capable of giving an inspiring performance on solo piano, unaccompanied by orchestra, and Tito was quite capable of thrilling an audience accompanied only by Ivor Newton.

The 'film star' tag still hung around Tito Gobbi's neck and he was approached to play in *The Glass Mountain*, co-starring the husband and wife duo, Michael Denison and Dulcie Gray.

The Yorkshire Evening Post played an important part in presenting the best music to the greatest number of people. They had the courage to finance big concerts, à la Proms, at

Leeds Town Hall. The newspaper was keen to show that Leeds was just as musical as anywhere else. London was well catered for, Bournemouth had an excellent orchestra, Huddersfield its Choral Society, Manchester had the Hallé, Durham University was famed for its Music Department, so, why not Leeds? This was before the prestigious Leeds International Piano Competition, nowadays acknowledged as one of the top four such competitions in the world, therefore, The Yorkshire Evening Post has much to be proud of in the world of music.

They found space in the paper for chit-chat about music and musicians and by this means the public became interested. Reporters and photographers on the Yorkshire Evening Post staff were sent to London to take pictures of the stars, one memorable picture being Paolo Silveri picking apples in Covent Garden.

Marguerite and Tito were engaged to perform with the Yorkshire Symphony Orchestra, conducted by Clarence Raybould.

The concert was a sell-out and it was repeated the next night.

This shows what a newspaper can do. It is sponsorship at its best.

The Wolff/Silveri concerts were a triumph, and the newspaper gave a splendid dinner afterwards.

The Yorkshire Evening Post had achieved its ambition, to show the country that Leeds *could* support celebrity concerts. Snippets from its editorials tell their own success story:—

'Today the "Evening Post" is able to announce Yorkshire's musical event of the year . . . a concert presented by this newspaper to hear the world's foremost performers. Impresarios in London have said that Leeds will not support celebrity concerts. We disagree emphatically.'

An earlier visit to Leeds by the famous singer Gigli had fallen through so the Yorkshire Evening Post had engaged Paolo Silveri for his first visit to Leeds, and, in the same programme, 'one of the most promising of our younger pianists and for whom a brilliant future is predicted . . . Marguerite Wolff'.

So Marguerite was already known to Yorkshire audiences and Lynford and Joel were extremely wise to engage her as partner to the newly-arrived Tito Gobbi. In its initial chit-chat about the first visit to Leeds by the young pianist, the Evening Post concluded with, 'she (Marguerite Wolff) has given recitals in London and Paris. Her last, in the French capital, was a sensational success.'

Apart from visits to Paris, Lynford and Joel kept Marguerite so busy performing at British concerts that there was hardly time to organise overseas tours.

ROYAL ALBERT HALL

(Manager - C. S. Taylor)

Monday Evening, May 16th, at 7.30

In aid of the
Catholic Workers'
London Scholarship Fund

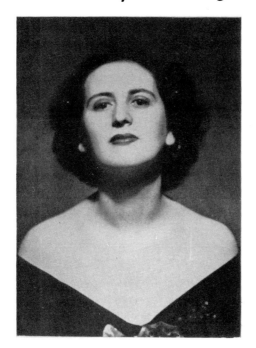

MARGUERITE
WOLFF

THE CELEBRATED PIANIST

AND

TITO
GOBBI

WORLD FAMOUS ITALIAN OPERA
AND FILM STAR

At the Piano : **IVOR NEWTON**

TICKETS :   2/6,   3/6,   5/-,   7/6,   10/-   **and**   12/6

On sale now at the Box Office, Royal Albert Hall (KEN. 8212); Chappell's, 50 New Bond Street, W.I
(MAY. 7600), and all usual Agents

Management :
LYNFORD-JOEL PROMOTIONS LTD., 17 Cavendish Square, W.I   (LANgham 3591)

Hot on the success of her Albert Hall debut with Tito, Marguerite was sent on an exciting series of concerts all over the British Isles.

Two-artist concerts were fashionable and among the celebrated stars who shared billing with Marguerite were, Josef Locke, Gwen Catley, Alfredo Campoli, Bill Johnson, Leon Goossens, Louis Kentner — and many others. There is no attempt at chronological order in the concerts listed here, and not all the concerts were arranged by Lynford and Joel.

Her recitals and broadcasts were tremendously popular, especially her playing of Liszt and Chopin. This, and her willingness to perform new works, established her reputation in Britain. She was always invited back, a typical report being one published in Eastbourne:—

'Marguerite Wolff was the solo pianist on the programme, and one has seldom heard Chopin better played. Her technique was brilliant and her interpretations sensitive. The applause she received made it clear that the Eastbourne audience will be glad to welcome her back to the concert platform in the not too distant future.'

Marguerite gave three concerts with Leon Goossens, the first being in Lincoln, with the two artists travelling there by train. A Mrs. Basch, a hostess who liked to introduce Marguerite to important people, was chief designer for the House of Worth. She said, 'Marguerite, when you travel with the great Leon Goossens you must wear something beautiful.' Mrs. Basch made a most enchanting little black suit and supplied the right hat and accessories, for Marguerite's meeting with Leon.

Thanks to the enthusiasm of Lynford and Joel, plus the professional contacts she had already made, Marguerite Wolff was busier than she had ever been, and life was a hectic kaleidoscope of concert-giving interspersed with necessary periods of practice and preparation.

A young amateur music impresario, Monty Hubbersgilt, generously organised music concerts, particularly at the Macabi Club in Hampstead, north London. Marguerite was engaged to play with Alfredo Campoli at one of these concerts and afterwards Monty suggested to her that she play the big *D Minor Piano Concerto No. 1* , by Brahms. This work is not usually included in the repertoire of lady pianists, and Marguerite's reply was, 'That's not a work I'd ever play, it isn't a woman's piece.'

Monty continued to support Marguerite, attending her concerts, and he became a welcome visitor to her home. He was

ROYAL
ALBERT
HALL
(Manager: C. S. Taylor)

SUNDAY
EVENING
NOVEMBER 28TH
AT 7 P.M.

IN AID OF THE
SAVE THE CHILDREN
FUND
Registered under the War Charities
Act, 1940

THE WORLD-FAMOUS CONDUCTOR
ARTUR
RODZINSKI

CONDUCTING THE
LONDON SYMPHONY ORCHESTRA
(Leader: GEORGE STRATTON)

SOLO PIANOFORTE:
MARGUERITE WOLFF

very persistent about Marguerite playing the Brahms *D Minor Concerto* until, eventually, Marguerite said, 'Well, if I were engaged to play it, I suppose I would accept.'

Seemingly this was the 'go-ahead' Monty had been waiting for because he immediately contacted Lynford and Joel and told them that he would finance a concert with Marguerite as soloist in the Brahms. Lynford and Joel shared Monty's confidence in Marguerite and the London Symphony Orchestra was engaged to play at the Albert Hall, with a super-star conductor. It was fortunate that Artur Rodzinski was free and he accepted the commission. The concert was arranged for a winter's evening, Sunday, November 28 at 7.00 p.m.

Marguerite Wolff began to study this mighty Brahms' concerto with Louis Kentner. Progress was excellent and Kentner knew that Marguerite had the technique, the strength, and the sensitivity to perform the work successfully. There were three months to prepare, not a great deal for a work of that scale. She worked fifteen hours a day and, Marguerite claims, she was 'completely terrified' of Artur Rodzinski. But, as all artists know, the 'terror' was the nervous reaction to the build-up for the big night. It was the impetus which drives the artist on in that elusive search for perfection. The artist views such a situation as just one more exciting and demanding adventure.

Things were going marvellously well; tickets were selling, there was confidence everywhere, and even the shattering news, one week before the concert, that Artur Rodzinski had gone down with double pneumonia and would not be able to conduct, did not immediately cause Lynford and Joel undue concern.

They quickly learnt, however, that world famous conductors cannot be booked at one week's notice. They tried, unsuccessfully, to engage someone of Rodzinski's standing. One such conductor, Leopold Stokowski, was busy but he offered his assistant, a young man called Leonard Bernstein.

Today, as we read this, we might be excused for thinking how very fortunate for Lynford and Joel that such an excellent man was available, but, at that time Bernstein was unknown outside the major American cities.

Bernstein had not yet written *West Side Story,* although his musical *On The Town* had shown New York something of his enormous potential. In November 1943 he had stepped in for Bruno Walter and conducted the New York Philharmonic Orchestra, receiving a standing ovation.

The war years had obscured his activities from the British public, so Lynford and Joel can be excused for deciding that Leonard Bernstein was, in Britain, comparatively unknown.

Then George Macnab, Dean of Westminster, a close friend of Marguerite's and a regular supporter of her concerts, had a seemingly excellent idea. Why not Louis Kentner? Kentner had expressed a desire to be a conductor, and what a wonderful story, 'Pianist conducts his pupil!'

Monty Hubbersgilt, who was financing the concert, knew that Louis Kentner would be a good draw with the crowds. The newspapers took up the story right away and Lynford and Joel, who were only acting as agents for Monty in this particular concert, and not as impresarios in their own right, went to see Louis Kentner who was giving a full recital of the Beethoven sonatas at the Winter Gardens, Drury Lane. The situation was now critical because the concert was almost on top of them.

Louis Kentner was approached during the interval of one of his Beethoven sonatas concerts and he asked to be allowed to play the *Waldstein* in the second half, and then he would discuss it.

When the position was explained one of his thoughts was, of course, not to let Marguerite down, so he accepted.

The concert was a sensation, although not quite in the manner anticipated by either Monty Hubbersgilt or by Lynford and Joel.

The day after the concert the sudden switch of conductors was front page news.

This is Marguerite's recollection of the affair.

'There were two rehearsals. Artur Rodzinski had insisted on this. Louis Kentner conducted both rehearsals, the second being on the Friday before the Sunday concert. Kentner cancelled a concert in order to conduct. For me the Friday rehearsal was perfect. Louis and I had worked together on the Brahms, so closely and so profoundly, we knew every note, every nuance, every change of tempo, and every bit of rubato. For me he was the perfect person to conduct, he knew every single thing I was going to do. To be actually conducted by your maestro is marvellous, and I derived great comfort from this. Our work together had grown to fruition for the concert.

'The full concert included the Schubert *Unfinished Symphony,* and the Beethoven *Fifth Symphony* which is, of course, notoriously difficult to conduct.

'There were a number of people in my Artists' Room before the concert. They left one by one, my mother wishing me "Good Luck!" and leaving me alone with Louis Kentner. We were discussing the finer points of the Brahms, but mainly for comfort, I am always nervous before a concert.

'Ten minutes before the concert was due to begin one of the London Symphony Orchestra committee came in and said,

Orchestra objects to Kentner

News Chronicle Reporter

LOUIS KENTNER, internationally famous as a virtuoso pianist, sat in a box at the Albert Hall last night and heard . . .

The announcement that he would be unable to conduct the London Symphony Orchestra at the Hall because fog had prevented his arrival from Bradford.

Ten minutes before a deputation of the players had told Kentner that they objected to his conducting on the " grounds of inexperience."

He remained in the hall for part of the programme to listen to one of his pupils, Miss Marguerite Wolf, play the Brahms Piano Concerto No. 1 solo.

One rehearsal

Afterwards Kentner told me: " I was engaged to conduct the concert, a week ago, in place of Artur Rodzinski, who is ill.

" We had a rehearsal on Friday, the only rehearsal, which I thought went very well, but after which I was not told anything at all.

" Tonight, ten minutes before I was due to begin, I was called on by three orchestra members who suggested that I let Mr. George Stratton, leader of the orchestra,

Kentner

conduct the two symphonies in the programme, and that I conduct only the Brahms concerto. The reason given was that I was not an experienced conductor.

" That was a well-known fact: they knew I was not experienced.

" I at once refused to conduct only the concerto. I told the deputation: ' In that case I won't conduct at all.'

" They gave out that I was delayed by fog, and Mr. Stratton conducted the whole programme. It was funny sitting and listening to the announcement. I suppose they had to give out something, though."

Kentner, a native of Hungary, is a brother-in-law of Yehudi Menuhin, the violinist.

"Oh, Mr. Kentner, can you spare us a moment in the conductor's room," so he went, and they closed the door.

'Then I heard the concert begin with the Schubert and, for me, everything was going to plan. I began to practise on the piano in the Artists' Room, and after about twenty minutes I thought "my time is approaching", and I powdered my nose and went outside the room, which led directly on to the platform.

'I saw an excitable scene. There was Louis Kentner, his mother-in-law Lady Harcourt, John Joel, and Monty Hubbersgilt. Kentner turned to me and said, "I'm sorry, my dear, but I'm letting you down!"

'They were putting the piano top up, and George Stratton, leader of the orchestra, came up to me and said, "Well, my dear, we're on!", and I went on with Stratton.

'Then, I sat at the piano, and the huge orchestral opening of the Brahms began — it is four or five minutes before the piano comes in. The orchestra played magnificently, they knew every nuance. Stratton conducted magnificently. After the performance, one hour long, there was a seething mass of reporters, all saying to me, "What happened? What happened?" and Lady Harcourt wringing her hands and saying, "Poor Louis, Poor Louis!", and Louis saying to me, "My dear, I let you down!". A man from Reuters was talking to me and all I could say was, "I don't know! I don't know!"

'Once I was on I was on. To play the Brahms was an enormous musical experience, you have to sit among it, it is absolutely shattering, I was swept on to the platform with Stratton, I knew nothing about the drama, but at the end I knew we'd played the Brahms successfully, and the orchestra and the audience knew.

'It was only later that I knew about the reasons for the sudden switch of conductor.' (The law case came one year later, R. C-L.)

Marguerite's sister, Dolly, summed it up with simple clarity when she said, 'Everything was a disaster, except the performance!'

'One of the many articles printed at the time. Every leading newspaper carried the story.'

Four

Four hundred guests attended the wedding reception of Miss Marguerite Wolff and Mr. Derrick Raymond Moss at the Trocadero Restaurant, Piccadilly. The marriage took place at the Hampstead Synagogue.

Less than a year had passed since 'The Brahms' and it was a period which had profoundly altered Marguerite's life. Immediately after the concert a courtesy aunt, Lily, had rung up to ask how one of Marguerite's aunts was, following a spell in hospital. Lily, who had not been at the Albert Hall concert but who had read the front page newspaper reports, was naturally very curious about the Louis Kentner affair and wishing to gain first-hand information she invited Marguerite for tea the following Sunday.

Marguerite accepted, never dreaming that she was to meet her future husband there.

Lynford and Joel then rang Marguerite to tell her that they had booked her to play the Tschaikovsky *Piano Concerto No. 1 in B flat minor,* in three weeks' time. As she had not played this work in public before and as she also had a recital in Paris in a week's time she knew she would now have to work every available minute to get her performance of the concerto up to the high standard she had always set for herself.

Marguerite never allowed anything to interfere with the practice time she considered necessary, and her close friends, male and female, appreciated this. Consequently it was in keeping with her own code of self-discipline that she decided the extra concert on hand made it imperative that she cancel Lily's invitation. She asked Dolly to ring up and explain. Dolly, for possibly the first time, refused to do her elder sister bidding.

'I told Marguerite to go. She was wearing a smart jacket over a jumper. At that time she was keen on fishnet tights and I told her she had a ladder, but she just went off,' Dolly explained.

'I remember I had a ladder in my stocking,' Marguerite recalls, 'but there was no time to change. Going to that tea party changed the whole course of my life'.

At the Sunday tea was Derrick Moss, listening intently to the facts of the 'Brahms' drama as Marguerite related them to Lily and the other guests. This dominated the afternoon's conversation. The opinions of some of the leading characters in the affair were, of course, mentioned. There were those who believed that Monty Hubbersgilt was in love with Marguerite. Louis Kentner's agreed fee had not been paid yet and there was speculation as to what that might lead to. It was true he had not conducted, but he had been there, willing to do so. Indeed, he had cancelled a concert in order to be at the Albert Hall. Monty Hubbersgilt was in contention with Lynford and Joel over the financial settlement of the concert and it was evident from what Marguerite was saying that the affair was far from over.

Marguerite had first met Derrick Moss when she was a teenager. At Lily's tea party she found him to be most charming, and she thought that he was a very attractive man, but she had no thought about seeing him again as she hurried home to get on with her practice.

No sooner had she closed the front door than the telephone rang.

It was Derrick Moss.

He invited Marguerite to go with him to the opera on the following Saturday evening.

Marguerite was playing in Paris on the Friday evening, and she had already decided that she needed every minute available for practice and final study of the Tschaikovsky concerto. With any of the men friends she knew, or had known in the past, she would have refused this particular invitation. But with Derrick she found herself accepting. In her mind she worked out that it would be possible to hurry back from Paris and meet Derrick as he was requesting.

What was it made Marguerite change her behaviour?

It is fitting at this point to mention the men friends in Marguerite's life because not one of them had ever done what Derrick was now doing, persuading her to keep an appointment when it meant breaking her own self-imposed discipline regarding practice and study.

Because of her charm and her beauty, together with the elegance of her music, Marguerite had attracted a certain kind of following. It is natural that from this following there should have been men who wanted to marry her. These friendships had, inevitably, been made in what might be termed the 'world of music'. Artists make many of their friends in 'after the concert' gatherings, and Marguerite was no exception to this way of life. This is how she had met many of the important people in her life.

On one such occasion Marguerite was giving a concert at St. George's Church, in Bloomsbury. She arrived early to try out the piano and do some practice. Her father and one of her piano pupils, Joyce Sinclair, were with her. They were met at the door by a drunken verger who refused to hand over the key because 'it wasn't time yet!' The argument was going on far too long for Marguerite's liking but when her father eventually produced some money the verger began to think that opening time at the church could conceivably coincide with opening time elsewhere. With signs now becoming optimistic Marguerite, not wishing to waste more time, hid behind a large tombstone. With Joyce on guard she quickly undressed and struggled into her concert attire.

That concert is not only memorable for the macabre tombstone dressing-room but also for an after-the-concert meeting.

RIL FIRST CONCERT!
chie Camden, Leon Goossens,
ndy Toye, M.W.,
nice Grayson.

61

Marguerite was taken to a funny little club in Bloomsbury, situated in a cellar. She sat at a wooden table, with one of the Dolmetsch family on one side, and a military-looking man on the other. Some little time later the military gentleman said that he would like Marguerite to play at his house.

Marguerite replied, 'I'd love to play at your house, but I don't know where you live,' so he handed her his card.

He was Sir John Forsdyke, Director of the British Museum.

The next morning he rang Marguerite and invited her to the Director's House at the British Museum. These became regular Sunday afternoon visits.

'He used to have China tea ready, and digestive biscuits, and he would always have a rare manuscript of Mozart or Haydn for me to look at.'

Marguerite then became a visitor to his ancient country house in Kent. On one occasion they were talking under a ripe plum tree and Marguerite happened to say what a wonderful colour for a concert dress. A short time later Marguerite received yards and yards of marvellous velvet, the same colour as the plums. When she played at a concert in The National Gallery she wore Sir John's plum dress because it blended beautifully with the décor.

Now, at another music club Marguerite met a very different type of man, not established and settled like Sir John, but a brilliant young conductor at the start of his professional career. This was David Ellenburg.

Marguerite met him at a politically-minded music club, with left-wing musicians, notably Alan Bush. Not all remained in the fold, of course. One good friend of Marguerite's, Solly Lawson, changed from Red to Blue, becoming a Conservative. A friend and musical colleague of David Ellenburg's, one Emanuel Young, although he would discuss politics he kept his musical life separate. David was not like that. He was an idealist, believing that he had been given his musical talents to use in 'spreading the word.'

It was his tremendous musical ability which attracted Marguerite to him. Had he kept to that, his relationship with her would have lasted longer than it did. He was a welcome visitor, for a time, at Marguerite's home but neither she nor her family were the least bit interested in David Ellenburg's lectures on Communism.

Dolly recounts, 'He used to corner mother, and she would patiently say, "Yes, David — yes David", but he was not put off by mother's indifference.'

There could not have been a greater difference between Sir John Forsdyke and young David Ellenburg.

But how to meet them both? Marguerite would not budge from her timetable of work. For a period of time the answer was to see Sir John on Sunday afternoon, and David on Sunday evening, and this is how she managed it.

Sir John in Love (he wrote beautiful letters to Marguerite when he was away) would see her to the eastern subway of Tottenham Court Road tube station. He would gallantly wave her 'Goodbye' with some romantic quotation, a favourite of his being Jessica's:

'. . . in such a night as this,
when the sweet wind did gently kiss the trees.'

In Shakespeare's play Shylock's lively daughter Jessica then meets her beloved Lorenzo in the avenue leading to Portia's house.

After leaving Sir John, Marguerite would emerge from Tottenham Court Road tube station by the western subway and meet young David who, in those days, was conductor of the Carl Rosa Opera Company. He would whisk Marguerite away for a Sunday evening stroll in Green Park.

'. . . in such a night as this,
when the sweet wind did gently kiss the trees
And they did make no noise.'
(Shakespeare. *Merchant of Venice*).

If the Green Park trees were silent Red David certainly was not. The affair came to its inevitable ending, because Marguerite had been enamoured with David and his music, but not with his politics.

Her affair with Sir John also ended because he wanted to marry Marguerite but she could not see marriage fitting into her life at that time.

Another suitor who was a great influence in Marguerite's life was Doctor 'Jaime' Arango the Colombian Ambassador in London. The friendship lasted for nearly four years and her family thought that Marguerite would marry and go to South America to live.

Marguerite had met the Ambassador at one of Mrs. Basch's parties. He introduced Marguerite to a highly sophisticated life style. Dr. Arango was very distinguished-looking, very courteous, and extremely talented, and Marguerite was very much enthralled. She found it exciting to mix with people who had truly established themselves, and they also gave her the adulation which young artists do need.

'The sound of the final chord dies away.'

'The audience responds with an ovation.'

'A', a Director of Entertainments and Music Organiser, in a letter to Marguerite, wrote:

'. . . I have had a very pleasant week travelling with Solomon. You were discussed. I can't imagine *why* I always seem to get you into the picture. Solomon said he remembered you playing to him and thought you were very promising and wished he could have had you as a pupil. I don't think you ever told me Solomon heard you. He is such a dear. He gave three recitals in the Ilfracombe area, and we stayed at The Imperial, Barnstaple. I tried to take him to the Harpers, but he absolutely refused to practise at all during the week. He said he was on holiday.

Had a nice time with Lou Lou (Louis Kentner) but don't think I was a very good deputy for Griselda! . . . do you?

I travelled a Blüthner round with Solomon, and I wished I could have done it for you as I consider your programme much more strenuous than Solomon's.

How is your Ambassador? (Dr. Arango). You haven't married him yet? I feel inclined to start a war with his country over you.

Well darling, I must go places and do some work. When am I to see you again? I had such a happy time at Barnstaple with you, in spite of your obvious craze for practising the piano. I really wished I were a piano.

Love. 'A'.

Before becoming an Ambassador Dr. Arango had been an international surgeon, and he had written an important book on the British contribution to Medicine.

He called Marguerite 'The Girl' and her nickname for him was 'Jamie'.

Dr. Arango, very much a man of the world, said, '"The Girl" flew into my life like a little bird . . . and one day she will fly away.'

And this is exactly what happened.

When Marguerite's engagement was announced Dr. Arango was deeply hurt, but he was a wise man and no doubt he remembered his own words. He returned to Colombia.

Of Marguerite's romances Dolly has this to say. 'Marguerite always had a string of followers. An extraordinary thing about her was that she created in her male admirers a very remarkable sort of worship, a fanatical sort of feeling for her.'

The following poem epitomises this devotional worship. (The writer's name is nowhere mentioned in this book.)

THOU HUMAN SYMPHONY
To Marguerite Wolff

I

How oft' am I to question — Marguerite —
'Who you are' and 'Where you come?'
How many sleepless nights am I to spend
Whilst listening to sweeping motifs say:—
Or stern:— Or brusque:— Or sweet:—
Or innocently mischievous:—
Each with the other to a mortal end
In combat wrought within thy tender breast?

———

Thou art a Symphony in Human Life and Love!
With Human brain and heart and gracious limb:—
Ne'er would I change this, Bless'd One! For indeed
The greatest music needs its singing lute
Or harp — Or trumpet — ere it may become
Express'd coherently unto each worldly soul.

———

Wert thou to stay Divine;— Divine alone:—
Could I, a worthless creature of this earth,
Whilst wrap't in dark morbidity and gloom,
Still harken to those deep, inspiring themes —
And harmonies — and rhythms — *that are you?*
I fear this could not be! And thus
I thank whatever God didst give thee flesh!

Sometimes when I address thee, Marguerite,
'Tis *not* a Fellow-Being with whom I speak:
There are deep rivers 'twixt us' — valleys too,
And mountain ranges unsurmountable!
There is fog to blind me — thick, thick fog —
To rob me of this oh! so beauteous vision!

––––––––––

But ne'ertheless of Womanhood thou art:
Human beyond belief:— But human still!
The laughter is the binding link between us, —
And what thou livest for I dare to love!
Is this a sin — my most Beloved One! —
To serve a great Ideal such as thee?

––––––––––

II

Thou tellest me thy heart remaineth whole.
Then in this, too, I stand in dire defeat;—
For mine was broken near two years ago —
One bleak November when I sail'd from thee:
Disgrac'd because I fell in human strife
Whilst thou wert still unblemish'd, pure and free!

––––––––––

My heart was broken when I sail'd away!
To foreign lands I travell'd:— and in each
I chanc'd to meet, maybe, a passing friend
To whom I pray'd, in silence, that they rob
Me of my agonising love for thee:
Alas! With violence did my soul repeat, —
'She is not Marguerite! — Oh! God above!
She is not Marguerite! — Not Marguerite!'

––––––––––

And then; — returning to my native shoes
I long'd — oh! how I long'd — to incarnate
The vision which had haunted me! But fear
Did intervene with His most deadly sword!
Again I heard that dreaded Voice exclaim:—
'No Marguerite for you! No Marguerite!'

––––––––––

I gazed ahead:— and felt that Death alone
Could now transcend the obstacles that stood,
Immovable, across my path of dreams:—
Oblivion the answer, after all? —
Until, once more, I heard the echo'd words
'She *may* forgive you! Yes, she *may* forgive!'

———————

Thou stoop'd to do this, Dearest One! And when
I heard thy voice again it seem'd as though
Some ancient Goddess freed me from a curse
Which damn'd my Heritage since Genesis!

———————

III

Thou givest music with those dainty hands:—
Thy fingers to command some raptur'd theme
Of genius — interpreted as none
But thee could e'er interpret it again!
And yet I question this: For I can hear
Far greater music in thy own sweet eyes!

———————

Could I but analyse those treasur'd sounds
That reach my ears when thinking, Love, of thee!
Alas! I cannot comprehend such depth
Of meaning which thy golden presence brings!

———————

Perchance I hear the drums of anger beat!
Perchance I hear a piano softly sing!
Or else, maybe, a giggling piccolo:—
These are your charms! O Fascinating One!
These are your charms! All these in you I hear!
In gravest wrath or in thy calmest mood
Such ecstasy for e'er shall dominate!

———————

Ah! How I love good music, — Marguerite, —
As written in the finest Symphony:—
Thou art that Symphony, O Marguerite!
Need I reason further? Need I?

———————

END

Throughout these young love affairs which came to nothing there was no fixed resolution in her mind that she would never marry. It was simply that she had not really met anyone with whom she wanted to spend the rest of her life. Then she met Derrick and everything was changed. Marguerite has tried to rationalise it since.

'After "The Brahms" I was tired, and I was receptive. There's a psychological time to get married. What triggers it off so often is the condition of the person at that particular time. It would have been different if I'd met Derrick while I was working on "The Brahms". When I did meet him it was at a time that I felt I wanted someone to rest on and lean on.'

Marguerite, being an artist, loves the feeling of being 'free as a bird', and also what she refers to as a 'sense of expectancy'.

'I think you've always got to have this high sense of expectancy. That part of life is an adventure. Where am I playing next? What is going to happen next? Who will I meet next? Being a performer is the most elegant form of casual labour, but there is something wonderful about it.'

Derrick was a very normal sort of man. His family led a stable existence and Marguerite saw another side to family life. Derrick, for his part, also saw how Marguerite's family lived.

The two young people became fascinated not only with each other but also with each other's background.

As Marguerite explains, 'My mother never minded if she cooked meals for us all at different times. We were all doing different things. For one of us it would be dinner at seven, another would come in two hours later and have it then, and someone else at another time. Derrick was fascinated with my mother's home. We might come in at ten and mother would say, "Do you want some dinner, darling?", but with his own mother it would be, "Do remember, Derrick, dinner is at a quarter past seven!", and it really was.'

Marguerite flew back from Paris and attended the opera at Covent Garden. Derrick, not a regular opera or concert-goer, had fortuitously made an excellent choice because that night Marguerite's friend, Paolo Silveri, was appearing with Elisabeth Schwarzkopf, in Verdi's *La Traviata*. Derrick met the stars, and then took Marguerite to the Savoy Hotel for dinner.

The next morning a perceptive Paolo Silveri rang Marguerite and asked, 'Who was that pretty boy I saw you with last night?'

In the days that followed, Marguerite, to please Derrick, did the things normal people like to do; going to the cinema and theatre, going for walks, and staying up late talking.

Marguerite usually went to bed early, but with Derrick she

The bride wore French satin-damask with V-neck and tight fitting bodice and long train. She wore her future mother-in-law's wedding veil, and a head-dress of orange blossom. Her flowers were orchids and gardenias.

never looked at the clock. She found him to be very magnetic and for the first time in her life the piano was taking second place. She should have been working on the Tschaikovsky, but her self-discipline in this respect was neglected.

She played the Tschaikovsky *Piano Concerto,* with the London Symphony Orchestra, and although she got a huge ovation she was secretly miserable with her own performance.

Marguerite's mother was delighted that her eldest daughter was being courted by Derrick. Nina had not been too happy over the Dr. Arango relationship but she was very happy to meet Derrick's family. She found them to be very distinguished, and absolutely charming. Derrick had two brothers, Albert and Lewis, and a sister, Eileen. His maternal grandmother was Lady Tuck.

Both families were fully supportive as it became more and more obvious that Marguerite and Derrick were forming a permanent relationship.

There were concerts and recitals to be fitted in during the first few months of the courtship and then came a summer concert, in Torquay, where Marguerite was again engaged to play the Tschaikovsky *Piano Concerto.* The whole of Derrick Moss's family decided to visit Torquay and hear Marguerite play. Grandpa Moss, a very distinguished-looking gentleman and sort of elder statesman of the family, joined the group, and they all booked into the Imperial Hotel. Marguerite was playing with the orchestra there.

Derrick suggested to Marguerite that it would be a pleasant thing to take it easy down to Torquay and break the journey. Hitherto this would have been an unthinkable waste of time for Marguerite. She would have got there as quickly as she could, begun her practice at the earliest opportunity, and returned home as soon as possible.

They had an idyllic journey from London to the coast, finding somewhere attractive to stay on the way, doing a little sunbathing, taking it easy in the afternoon, and staying up late.

'I suppose I wanted to show Derrick I was an ordinary person. It is amazing what you do when you want to please someone. You smother a lot of things you don't think the other side is going to like.'

The concert went well as far as Derrick's family was concerned, and the audience was well pleased, especially as Marguerite and Derrick announced their engagement. The local Press headlined the concert report with, 'Her Greatest Engagement.' Then the National Press reported the engagement, referring once more to the Albert Hall affair, 'Miss Wolff was the pianist in the

Albert Hall concert in which the orchestra refused to play with Mr. Louis Kentner as the conductor.'

Despite the applause of the audience and the obvious delight of Derrick's family Marguerite was far from satisfied with her second performance of the Tschaikovsky *Piano Concerto*. She remembers that performance as being fairly crude and lacking the finer details, due, of course, to poor preparation on her part.

After the wedding ceremony Marguerite and Derrick honeymooned in Italy, knowing that on their return there was to be a court case between Lynford and Joel versus Monty Hubbersgilt, with Marguerite as a principal witness.

Grandpa Moss, Dolly, Walter, Derrick, Lily Moss, Lewis Moss, Arthur Walford, Nina, Howard Elton, Marguerite, Penelope Walford and Heather Tessler.

In his book John Joel writes, '. . . because of the fiasco, Hubbersgilt decided not to honour his guarantee, and we had to sue him for our losses which amounted to £545.'

(During the honeymoon Derrick and Marguerite met Cecil Wilson, the Daily Mail critic, and Wilson mentioned that he had been at the Friday rehearsal and there had been no L.S.O. objection to Kentner then).

Almost a year had passed since the concert and Monty was ill-advised to proceed. The case went to the Old Bailey, the judge being Justice Slade. Many of Marguerite's musical friends and supporters were there; Countess Winchelsea, Mrs. Lionel de Rothschild (these two supporters had sat together at Marguerite's first Lynford and Joel Wigmore Hall concert), Sir William Dale, George Macnab (who had suggested Louis Kentner) and his wife Crystal, Admiral John Godfrey, and others.

John Godfrey, whose wife was Neville Chamberlain's sister, was Head of Naval Intelligence during the war, his aide being Ian Fleming, writer of the James Bond stories. John loved going to concerts and was a great supporter of Marguerite's. He particularly liked the short period in the Artists' Room after a concert, calling it 'The Adoration of the Artist.' On that point, Clifford Curzon, the concert pianist, said that it was the one bit of pleasure an artist gets — the ten minutes after a concert, surrounded by family and friends, and before the artist reads the critics.

Each day during the week of the trial John Godfrey and Crystal Macnab took Marguerite for lunch at Simpsons in the Strand.

There was one point in the case where Harry Dugarde, chairman of the L.S.O., had implied that engaging Louis Kentner was a stunt, and the L.S.O. did not lend itself to stunts.

In the witness box this was put to Marguerite and she replied, 'If it was a stunt it was a stunt with a profound musical foundation.'

Marguerite's answer was taken very seriously, and when Reginald Vaughan, counsel for Lynford and Joel, reminded Dugarde that the L.S.O. had recently been conducted by a boy of ten (Roberto Benzi), the orchestra's objection to Kentner began to look rather stupid.

Lynford and Joel were awarded £515. Monty Hubbersgilt's bill for the case ran into several thousand pounds, and there was a rumour that he had to mortgage his house to settle this.

Monty had been happy at the outset to agree to cover all the expenses of the concert. His change of heart after concert coincided with Marguerite's love affair with Derrick. One can

Roberto Benzi

only hope that the two happenings were not related. Monty did not have a very strong case and he was very unwise to take it to court.

Derrick and Marguerite found an elegant flat, at the corner of Bramham Gardens and Earls Court Road. It was very spacious, and had a large drawing room, ideal for Marguerite to do her piano practice in. When Derrick had proposed marriage Marguerite had mentioned her musical life and he had said that he saw no reason why it should not continue.

There was plenty of time available for Marguerite to practise because Derrick worked long hours establishing his business. He had been in the Forces for seven years, mainly in The Middle East, and on his return to civilian life he spent the first year working for his old firm of Estate Agents. He then formed his own Estate Agency, subsequently bringing in his younger brother, Lewis Moss. Derrick drove himself. He had an extremely wealthy grandfather who did not believe in giving financial help to his younger relatives. He was of the opinion that they should make their own way, and this is what Derrick was determined to do. His office was at 17 South Moulton Street, and with his brother he built up a wonderful reputation for complete integrity, and the business became a huge success.

Marguerite found that she could practise exactly the same as before her marriage. It seemed almost too good to be true. She was particularly fortunate in her immediate neighbours.

Next door was Judge Campbell, and he was deaf. Below was an elderly lady and she, too, was deaf. To complete a perfectly suitable trio of adjacent neighbours Marguerite had in the flat above a Madame Anna Schouvaloff, and she was a music lover. Marguerite has always considered how fortunate *she* was to have the support and encouragement of Anna, possibly not realising how much the sound of piano practice meant to Anna Schouvaloff at that time.

Anna was born in Russia but some years after the Revolution she went to France for three years before deciding to make England her home. In London she met a fellow-Russian, Count Schouvaloff, and when they both became naturalised British subjects, in 1933, they married. Her husband was working in films as an Art Director (he won an American Award for his Art work in *Henry V,* and an Oscar in 1953, for *Moulin Rouge,* the Daily Telegraph critic reporting that even if the acting was poor 'the film would be worth seeing just for the exciting Art work') and as the technicians had trouble pronouncing and spelling his name, the former Russian Count changed his professional name to Paul Sherriff.

When Marguerite and Derrick became neighbours of Anna's she had her sick brother, Artemy, staying with her. Artemy was a fine singer. Before his illness he had sung, to give just one example, at a Dolmetsch Festival in Haselmere.

To complete Anna's artistic background her son, Alexander, on completion of his National Service, joined the Theatre Museum of the Victoria and Albert Museum, the world-wide collection now being housed at the Covent Garden precinct, where the old market used to be.

Allied to this artistic background Anna experienced what all humans feel from time to time, the emotional pull of one's birthplace. She loved England, she brought her son up as a normal English boy but, as with most people away from the land of their birth, there were memories of childhood. Marguerite's music was like manna from Heaven.

'It was wonderful to hear the music coming up into our room. I am sure Marguerite did not realise how much her music meant to me, or to my brother, a very fine singer, but who was sick at the time. Marguerite's practice was no ordinary practice. She never lost her finesse. For most people domesticity and family responsibilities blunt the artistic edge. Marguerite never lost her great and natural nobility. She organised the family life and her music so that everything seemed to work effortlessly. Her music helped me spiritually, it helped me to settle in my adopted country.

'Marguerite was the most generous person I ever met. She helped many people, morally and financially. I don't think she realised the important part she played. She was such a genuine person, and she was always sensitive to other people's feelings.

'I was very fond of her husband Derrick, and Marguerite did everything she possibly could to please him. The two little girls were very lovely, and they called me "Auntie". They were a delightful family.'

Anna Schouvaloff, now a widow, lives near to the mansion flats where she first met Marguerite. She never misses a Marguerite Wolff London-based concert.

One of the first major concerts after Marguerite's marriage required her to play the Tschaikovsky *Piano Concerto*. Although her two previous performances of this work had been public successes Marguerite herself had been far from satisfied. She now had the facilities and the mental resolve to especially give of her best in this particular work.

Another reason for Marguerite's determination to perform at her best was the fact that many of her relatives and friends were saying that she would lose interest in the piano now that she was married.

'This infuriated me and it egged me on. I practised enormously . . .'

The performance of the Tschaikovsky, that tremendously popular *Piano Concerto,* was the success Marguerite had striven for. Walter Goehr, the conductor, was lavish in his praise, stating that the Slow Movement was particularly well performed. He said to Marguerite that she 'played it like a Russian fairy tale'. The Press reviews were also excellent.

Artists will know that sometimes they can feel as if they are wafted out of themselves . . . they experience this sort of elevation, it's a sort of magic. Athletes, too, can experience this rare feeling of super-excellence, giving that special performance which is a grade better than their normal best.

Marguerite felt like this after her performance.
'It's magic when it happens. I think you're as near to Heaven as you will get on this earth. I look back on that performance with a sort of glow. I felt I played better than Nature intended me to.'

Walter Goehr

In the Artists' Room afterwards it was like old times, with old friends. Admiral John Godfrey was there, George and Crystal Macnab, Lady Winchelsea, Sir William Dale, many other people important in Marguerite's life, her family and, of course, her husband Derrick.

Marguerite became a superb organiser and with carefully thought out efficiency in her daily timetabling she found that she could run a home and have a profession. She was happy to be back on the concert platform even though the engagements were not at the hectic frequency of her pre-marriage days.

She remembers one particularly lovely concert, at the home, near Exeter, of her friend Mrs. Lionel de Rothschild. The Kathleen Riddick (all ladies) orchestra and Marguerite played in the open air, under a gorgeous magnolia tree. The programme included a work by Bach for piano and strings, and a rarely-played piece by the Spanish composer Joaquín Turina, *Rapsodica Sinfónica.*

Not many people thought that Marguerite could become domesticated. Her husband was rather anxious about this,

MEET A MIRACLE
MOTHER-TO-BE
Take a good look at the girl
above. She's one in 10,000.
She is Professor — yes,
PROFESSOR —
Marguerite Wolff, the concert
pianist. And that slim waist
measures just 22 inches, in spite
of the fact that she is expecting a
baby in two months' time.
Doctors say the odds against a
mother-to-be keeping her figure
like this are 10,000 to one.
The baby, they expect, will weigh
about six or seven pounds.
Only three weeks ago she gave
a recital in London. She is a
professor of the Trinity
College of Music.

but Marguerite took it as a challenge. She had always loved
entertaining so now she began giving dinner parties for eight,
ten, and sometimes a dozen or more people. Most of the
preparation she did the night before. She would also wash up at
night so that, more or less unknown to anyone, she could have
time during the day to do her prescribed amount of practice.
With this strict timetabling she managed to make everything
seem effortless.

Gradually, however, Derrick's enthusiasm for his wife's
music-making became directed towards her playing at home
to invited guests rather than playing in public. At the time
Marguerite felt a slight resentment but she now says, 'I suppose
it was only natural. Like any husband he wanted me for himself.'

Derrick's business was expanding and prospering and
Marguerite declared that, 'two years went delightfully by', and
then she found herself pregnant.

Marguerite continued giving concerts for seven months before
making the announcement of the impending birth. Only her
husband and their respective parents had known from the start.
She had always been very healthy and she felt quite well until
very late in the pregnancy. At seven months she gave a recital at
Wigmore Hall, and after this concert the announcement was
made.

Because her waist still measured 22 inches one newspaper
headlined her as a 'Miracle Mother-to-be.' She had not suffered
the usual aches and pains of pregnancy but, once it was officially
announced, on came the uncomfortable aspects; the heartburn,
headaches, nausea, insomnia . . . .

She gave birth to a daughter, Crystal.

Marguerite became an excellent housewife, a wonderful
mother, and loving wife and . . . by carefully organising her time
so that her responsibilities did not suffer, she managed to get in
her practice and keep her concert engagements.

Another two years passed and Marguerite began to carry her
second child. Once again the pregnancy did not show and it was
not until the seventh month that the news was made public.
Of course, if a woman is going to virtually ignore the pregnancy
then she was to behave in keeping and not expect special
considerations when feeling below par. Eventually Marguerite
did have to cancel a concert and retire until the birth. The concert
happened to be one of those given at H.M. Prison (either
Wormwood Scrubs or Wandsworth) arranged by Zenia Field
and Countess Winchelsea. Marguerite could not resist making
the obvious pleasantry that she did not want her baby to be born
in prison.

76

She gave birth to a daughter, Gloria.

The birth, however, coincided with a very sad occurrence affecting Marguerite's professional life. Lynford and Joel went out of business.

They had arranged a tour of British theatres for the French cabaret and film star, Maurice Chevalier, and this proved to be disastrous for the young impresarios. Maurice Chevalier had been a British box office hit before the war but the young post-war audiences were not impressed, and the middle-age Chevalier supporters were tied to their homes and families. At £450 a day and playing to half-empty theatres all over Great Britain, Maurice Chevalier ran up such gigantic losses for Lynford and Joel that they had to cease business.

John Joel telephoned Derrick who, knowing how upset Marguerite would be, waited a day or two until after Gloria had been born before breaking the news to Marguerite. She was, of course, terribly sorry for them. They had done so much for her career. As Dolly said, they were able to create so many glamour concerts. In the short time they lasted they were exciting impresarios.

A WAIST TO BE ENVIED

Marguerite Wolff, a concert pianist, is due to have a baby next month . . . but looking at her no one would have guessed it.

For attractive Marguerite — in private life Mrs. Derrick Moss — only six weeks before the baby is due — has a waist measurement of 23 inches — only two inches larger than it was a year ago.

And she is as trim of figure as a girl of eighteen.

Nor does the "unusualness" stop at that. Said Marguerite, putting on a last dab of make-up at her Earls Court Road flat before dashing off to join her husband at a New Year party:

"My first baby, Crystal Rose, is two years old. She was born a month ahead of time. The waist was the same then as it is today.

RESTING? — NO FETISH
"This time even mother didn't know — until, a few weeks ago, I told her."

Is there a secret of the Wolff waist? Said Marguerite: "I don't know of any. Maybe it's just the way I'm built, or perhaps my muscles are stronger than most women's.

"Exercise may have a bit to do with it of course. I don't believe in resting — at least not in making a fetish of it.

"The only concession I have made has been to cut my daily practice from eight hours to five, although, of course, I cancelled my concert engagements.

"Imagine how I felt when I had to refuse an invitation to play at a concert over Christmas. It was so worrying, having to explain.

"But the concert was to have been held in a prison — and if anything had gone wrong my baby would have been born in jail."

The Sydney Adamson portrait records a solemn study of Marguerite, but at the piano with her daughter Crystal, it is all smiles. (Sydney Adamson aged 84, also painted a picture of Crystal and Gloria together).

Marguerite and Derrick were in complete agreement over the education of their two daughters. Picture taken on Gloria's first birthday.

AT AVENUE ROAD.
Gloria, Marguerite, and
'Velvet' who, unlike 'Lisa',
did have a pedigree.

Dorothea, (Nanny), Cat,
no pedigree, named 'Lisa',
after Shaw's *Pygmalion*.

With two daughters to bring up Derrick was keen to give Marguerite all the help he could and a Miss Campbell was engaged. Marguerite, appreciating that Derrick came from a perfectly run home, was able to produce the smooth efficiency he expected. Marguerite succeeded because she had a certain type of stamina, not so much a physical strength, but rather one which contained an enormous staying power. This, allied to a warm and generous love, created a happy and efficient family, and one wherein Marguerite could continue with her music.

As Marguerite rightly says; 'There are various ways we can love; the love for a husband, the love for a child, and the love of doing what we have always done and have always loved doing.' Referring to those who said that marriage and motherhood would rob her of her desire to play, Marguerite declared, 'I could not see why people thought that because you had normal functions and normal life you would stop wanting to do what you had done all your life. The men pianists don't stop, why should the women?'

With his business expanding Derrick was able to plan more domestic help for his wife, the most important of which was Dorothea, nanny for the two little girls. Dorothea was twenty-four when she went to Marguerite, and she stayed for seventeen years. The only reason she left was to nurse her own mother, and that meant going to Austria. (When Crystal married, Dorothea came to England for the wedding).

Marguerite cannot speak too highly of Dorothea and of the wonderful influence she was on Crystal and Gloria.

'She was well educated and cultured, and she was a very beautiful lady.'

Marguerite and Derrick were in complete agreement over the education of their two daughters.

The girls started their school life at the Lycée Française in South Kensington, mainly because Marguerite and Derrick wanted their daughters to be bi-lingual. They would have gone right through at the Lycée but Derrick bought a grand house in Avenue Road, near Primrose Hill, Regent's Park, and this meant the family moving from the Earl's Court mansion flat where they had lived for nearly a decade.

It was a magnificent house, with seventeen rooms, and Derrick employed a permanent staff of four. He was a devoted father, a wonderful husband, and as a family man he had done all he could for them.

When the family moved into their new home the children went to the Town and Country School nearby. There was great emphasis in the curriculum on French and Music. The two girls walked to school, and back, accompanied by their nanny.

Marguerite did as many concerts as she could fit in with her busy family life and with her growing children. For some concerts she gave duets with her sister Dolly, which were extremely successful.

Dolly, too, was married by now, and when she became pregnant she emulated her elder sister by keeping the matter secret for almost seven months. It was at this time that Marguerite asked her to turn the pages for her at a Wigmore Hall concert.

'I sat as near to the piano as I could, but each time I leaned forward to turn a page I had to be careful not to press the bass notes of the piano down. It must have looked very odd.'

Marguerite and Derrick had been married fourteen years when one particular invitation to play at a concert arrived. It was from Shirley Rodwell, on behalf of Lady Bliss, wife of Sir Arthur Bliss, Master of the Queen's Musick, asking Marguerite if she would play at a charity concert for the Westminster Society for Mentally Handicapped Children. Marguerite wrote back, agreeing to play, and suggesting that it might be a good idea to add to the programme an item for 'four hands on one piano' with her sister, Dorothy Wolff. Lady Bliss wrote back saying how pleased she and Sir Arthur were with the idea.

A very short time after this Marguerite, still an early-riser, was talking to Dolly on the telephone. She then realised that Derrick was still in bed when normally he would have been up.

The previous evening (a Sunday) they had been watching television and Derrick had said to her that he felt rather tired and did she mind if he went to bed early.

When she spoke to him there was no reply. She saw that his arm was out of the bed and it was a purple colour. Marguerite thought he was sleeping and spoke to him again. Maria, the Portuguese maid, came into the bedroom and Marguerite said to her, 'Look at Mr. Moss's colour.'

Maria raised her hands and screamed, 'He's dead!'

Shocked — Marguerite telephoned for the doctor, and he arrived within minutes.

Five

After the funeral, Marguerite's brothers-in-law, Albert and Lewis, were marvellous to her. They offered any help or support she might need, and both said that she ought to get back on to the concert platform. Only with an activity as big as that could she hope to fill some of the void left by Derrick's sudden death. He had been an excellent and loving husband and father, a dynamic and magnetic force, and he had created not only a magnificent and prosperous business but also a lively social background for his family.

He had been, really, a rather shy man and had benefitted greatly from Marguerite's ability to meet and mix with people from many walks of life.

Marguerite's own family; parents, brother and sister, were also supportively on hand. She and the two girls derived a valuable sense of security from this affectionate family concern for their well-being.

Derrick had left Marguerite comfortably off, but Death Duties were a serious burden. Life was very difficult for her, living on a taxed income and running a big house with a staff of four. Some legal complications required Marguerite to stay at Avenue Road for a period of time, but one way and another she managed.

Marguerite believes that Crystal grew up almost overnight when Derrick died. For a little girl who had never even crossed the road on her own she showed that she possessed commendable initiative, in many ways. That she was ready to take on responsibilities was evident even on the day of the funeral. Because so many people came back to the house she quietly slipped out to buy some extra cakes. This was a small incident, of course, but indicative of her immediate realisation that as the eldest daughter she now had to help her mother to manage the family affairs, and her sense of responsibility was established then.

Crystal was eleven at the time and remembers feeling this responsibility. Losing her father made her aware that she could never take things for granted. The unexpected could always be just round the corner.

Crystal

Realising that widowhood cast a heavy burden on her mother, Crystal would have been happy if Marguerite had re-married.

The piano was always in Crystal's life and she cannot remember not hearing her mother playing. Music was Crystal's first language.

Nevertheless, having witnessed the discipline of her mother practising ten hours a day she did not feel that she had that sort of dedication. She decided to take up acting because this involved people rather than practising on one's own for hours on end.

Crystal admires her mother's flair for entertaining, her excellent dress sense, and her taste in décor, and these have been a big influence.

There is also a philosophy which Crystal has learnt from her mother, and that is that whatever drive or ambition you may have, the motivation must come from yourself.

Gloria was, of course, even younger but she, too, accepted new responsibilities when her father died. She grew to follow her own career into a more academic field than her sister. She is a first-class pianist but, like Crystal, she prefers other paths than those of the concert pianist.

The two girls, with their mother, thus adapted themselves into the life of a one-parent family.

The advent of the Lady Bliss concert was immeasurably significant because it gave Marguerite an immediate concert to prepare for and also, because of the association with Sir Arthur, a new music to study — the piano music of Arthur Bliss.

Marguerite says, 'The concert for Lady Bliss and the consequent meeting with Sir Arthur became an enormous thing in my life. Derrick's sudden death was terrible, but the pattern of life is strange. Sir Arthur was marvellous. He was everything a Master of The Queen's Musick should be, and a friendship started.'

Louis Kentner called on Marguerite to offer his condolences, and she was then more than pleased to renew her maestro-pupil relationship with him.

Marguerite was invited to the beautiful home of Sir Arthur and Lady Bliss, in St. John's Wood, London.

She also met the composer at one of the soirées given by Sir Basil and Lady Lindsay-Fynn at their home in Avenue Road. Sir Basil was Chairman of the Friends of Malta Society and he was eager for Marguerite to play there, and to make arrangements with the Chairman of the Society in Malta, Lady Mamo.

Peter Davis, who was a member of the British Council, London, suggested that Marguerite did a tour of Finland.

For both these overseas tours a British work was required and as Sir Arthur Bliss was present he was asked if he could recommend such a work. It was suggested that Marguerite play his *Piano Sonata*, and she readily accepted and agreed to work with the composer in preparing it for public performance.

At home in his music studio they analysed the work, and Sir Arthur gave Marguerite certain corrections, added bits, and gave detailed instructions. The slow movement is excessively slow and he instructed Marguerite, 'Immediately you have finished the first movements, place your hands ready for the slow movement, and wait, count eight crotchets, to prevent the audience applauding, then begin.'

This is stagecraft. Sir Arthur knew exactly what he wanted,

Sir Arthur Bliss

not only in his piano music but in each of the full range of his compositions.

Arthur Bliss was, of course, an excellent pianist, having studied with Ursula Creighton, herself a pupil of Busoni. Bliss was also an excellent judge of pianists, having been, for example, on the panel of the 1938 Ysaye International Competition for pianists.

His *Piano Sonata* had been written for the pianist Noel Newton-Wood but Noel commited suicide in 1953, and the work had been shelved. Marguerite became absorbed in the music of Arthur Bliss and added it to her concert repertoire. With enormous help from Louis Kentner, and with continued guidance from the composer himself, Marguerite studied the Bliss *Piano Sonata* in depth. When she performed it in public it became evident that she was becoming not only a skilled exponent of Bliss's piano music, but also something of a disciple. She was taking his music to a new audience, especially overseas. Concert organisers were quick to request that she included the Bliss *Piano Sonata* in her programme.

Other concert pianists also began to take an interest in the Bliss *Piano Sonata,* and thus the popularity of the work grew.

When it had become an established item in Marguerite's repertoire, and concert organisers were asking her to include it in her programmes, she, under the personal supervision of Sir Arthur, made the first recording of the work.

On the sleeve of the record Sir Arthur wrote:—

BLISS SONATA
Moderato marcato
Adagio sereno
Allegro

'This piano Sonata was the first work I composed for solo piano since an early collection of short pieces written in the mid-twenties. It was written as a "thank you" present for the late Noel Newton-Wood, who had given many splendid performances of my piano concerto. The Sonata was completed in 1952. The work is in three movements: the first of these starts with a stately rhythm, which recurs many times throughout the movements. The mood is of a somewhat steely brilliance, set off by a flowing lyrical section, which does duty for the classical second subject groups of the Sonata's first movement. I have marked the second movement "slow and serene"; it is conceived in "variation form"; it ends slowly and peacefully. The last movement is gay and lively. It presents some difficult technical problems to the player, and it closes in a fiery burst of sound.

Miss Marguerite Wolff has broadcast the Sonata from Helsinki and from Valetta, Malta, and has included it in her recitals in Lisbon, Rome and London.'

Arthur Bliss.

Also on the record sleeve is an appreciation of Marguerite Wolff, written by Robert Collet, and it includes the following:

'The detailed preparation which goes into every one of her performances is amply demonstrated on this new record (Academy ACM 1. Distributed by Davjon Limited, 67 Upper Berkeley Street, London W1) and we are proud to have the combination of the music of Sir Arthur Bliss and the great talents of Miss Marguerite Wolff.'

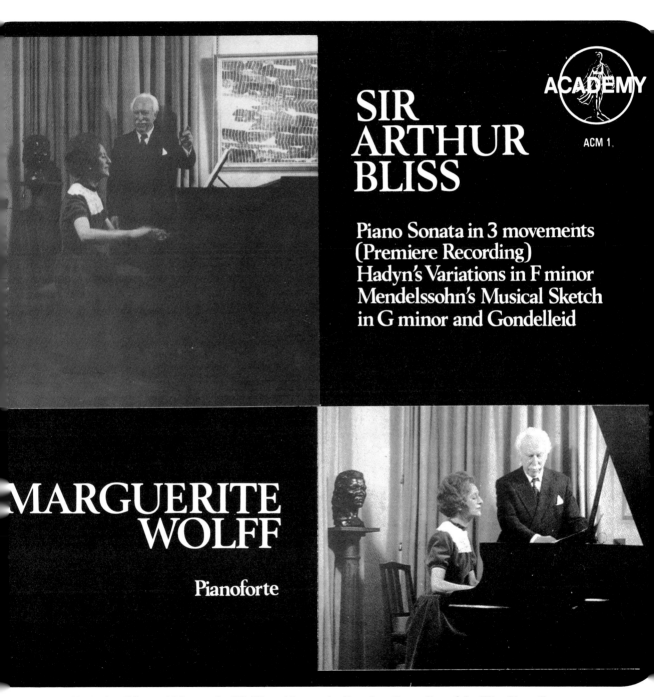

SIR ARTHUR BLISS

ACADEMY

ACM 1.

Piano Sonata in 3 movements (Premiere Recording)
Hadyn's Variations in F minor
Mendelssohn's Musical Sketch in G minor and Gondelleid

MARGUERITE WOLFF

Pianoforte

Sir Arthur Bliss and Marguerite Wolff working on the Premiere Recording of the Bliss *Piano Sonata.*

On the front of the record sleeve are two photographs of Sir Arthur Bliss working with Marguerite at the piano, in his own music room.

It is a beautiful recording of the sonata, the recording supervisor being Derek Faraday.

Marguerite's preference for make of piano is the Steinway. She has three at her home (but more of pianos and pianists later). When explaining some of the intricacies of the Bliss *Sonata*, Marguerite makes mention of the use of the Steinway middle pedal. Not all pianos have three pedals. Marguerite is referring to pianos which do have this third, and central, pedal.

This special pedal can sustain a note or chord while other notes are being played and the sustaining pedal (right foot) is being used in the normal fashion.

'Use of the middle pedal goes right through the work, but especially in the first movement. It is surprising the number of pianists who do not use the middle pedal. In this sonata its use is very important.'

Marguerite had already given one tour of Malta, so she was particularly welcome there when the occasion of playing the Bliss *Sonata* arrived. It was part of an international television conference, and Sir Arthur and Lady Bliss were also present on the George Cross island (Sir Arthur was there to conduct a concert).

An imaginative Maltese TV producer designed a beautiful set for the performance of the Bliss *Sonata*. Marguerite arrived early, to be followed by Sir Arthur and his party. When it was time to begin he said to Marguerite, 'Now, my dear, you will have to forgive me if I leave you. I have to introduce the sonata, and then I will introduce you, but then I have to go. I will watch the performance on TV tonight.'

Sir Arthur Bliss made the appropriate announcements, then he smiled at Marguerite and departed. He had been sitting in a chair at the end of the studio. The cameras were wheeled to the 'piano end', and Sir Arthur was nowhere in sight.

The relief to Marguerite was tremendous because television on its own is a tense enough situation for a performer and it would have been that much more so had the composer himself been there.

Signals were passed between the technicians, the red light went on, and Marguerite started to play.

The work takes about half-an-hour to perform. When she finished, the red light went off and, hurrying towards Marguerite, was Sir Arthur. He had stayed in the studio the whole time, but had kept out of sight, knowing Marguerite would feel freer if she believed he was not there. He embraced her, and congratulated her. This was an example of Arthur Bliss' great understanding of the artist.

Subsequently both Sir Arthur and Lady Bliss watched the TV programme from an ordinary bar in Malta. Later that evening the Governor General, Sir Maurice and Lady Dorman, gave a dinner party at the Palace on the island. Among the guests were Mrs. Vaughan Williams, Sir Anthony and Lady Mamo, the composer and Lady Bliss, and Marguerite.

Marguerite now began to play the Bliss *Sonata* everywhere, and it was prominently featured in her tour of Finland.

This tour was highly compressed, with sixteen concerts in fifteen days. Marguerite considers Finland to be not only extremely beautiful, with its glorious forests and mountains, but also highly civilised.

The centrepiece of the recitals was the Bliss *Sonata*, and this work was also broadcast and televised by Marguerite.

She chose to travel by train in Finland despite her love of flying. It would have been necessary to rise at 3.00 a.m. for a 6.00 a.m. flight, and that could have been disagreeable and tiring after one concert, and sometimes two, the day before. Travel by train meant that she could make use of the comfortable sleeping compartments and thus not waste time or lose any sleep.

The British Council arranged this Finnish tour and Marguerite was met at Helsinki by an official of the British-Finnish Society, and also Sir David and Lady Scott-Fox, the British Ambassador, who invited Marguerite to give a concert at the British Embassy. It was here that Marguerite met the sculptress who made the Sibelius monument. This was a work of enormous dimension; heavy manual work indeed for a lady. 'The cutting, hewing, chopping and shaping work involved, has changed my own shape,' laughed the very stocky sculptress.

Marguerite's next tour was in Portugal, playing in Lisbon, Oporto, and some smaller towns and cities. Wherever she played there was always waiting a telegram of good wishes from Sir Arthur Bliss. *

Because it was a new work, the Bliss *Sonata* aroused positive reactions from the various audiences who heard the work for the first time. Some liked it, but it was inevitable that there were others who showed disapproval.

In Oporto there were two ladies of tremendous importance and influence. These were Dorothy Tate and her sister Muriel,

* Telegram to Helsinki:
MARGARETE WOLFF CHEZ KAI MASSALO OY YLEIS RADIO FABIA NINKATU HLS. LOVE AND GOOD WISHES. ARTHUR AND TRUDY.

and they owned a great deal of land and property. They were genuine eccentrics, but they had an aura about them. Dorothy was the dominant sister. At the end of the Bliss Sonata, Dorothy Tate made no disguise of her anger. Later, at the reception Marguerite said, 'Miss Tate, I don't think you liked the sonata.'

She replied, 'My dear, I didn't only dislike it, I loathed it!'

Muriel said nothing. That was the relationship between the sisters.

Dorothy Tate's opinion was very much a minority view. The Portuguese Press wrote:

'Marguerite Wolff's worth as a pianist is undeniable. The study of Bliss's intricate sonata alone brings with it innumerable difficulties of all kinds such as to daunt all but the few. We enjoyed the work itself at first hearing, and although we did not find it as clear as Mozart, its modernism is not of a kind to make it incomprehensible to the ordinary listener; in fact, it can scarcely be considered modern nowadays.'

This report is remarkably astute. Marguerite is not a 'modernist', but she plays contemporary music, of her own choice. If we think of the piano music of, say, Liszt and Chopin as being 'romantic', and if we consider Bliss's statement, 'I am often told that I am a "romantic" composer. I have not the remotest idea what is implied by that definition,' it is clear that terminology can be misleading. As the French say, 'Give a thing a name and it loses half its beauty.'

There was nobility and a certain austerity about Arthur Bliss, possibly as a result of his military and public school background. But there was the human factor, or, to call it by a common name because of its common bond, a 'romantic streak'. This is one of the esoteric factors which makes a particular work of art appeal to a great number of people.

In 1929 Bliss wrote *Serenade,* and it was dedicated to his American wife, Gertrude. He writes:

'The idea for this *Serenade* came to me one day in 1929, as I sat in a gallery looking at a picture (was it a Fragonard?), in which a pleasure-loving group frolicked in one of those romantic gardens with temples and grottos, so favoured in the XVIIIth century.'

For this work Bliss revived the tradition of the vocal serenata. A singer sings a setting of Spenser's Sonnet, *Fair is my love,* in the 2nd of the four movements.

> Fair is my Love, when her fair golden hairs
> With the loose wind ye waving chance to mark;
> Fair, when the rose in her red cheeks appears;
> Or in her eyes the fire of love does spark.
> Sonnet LXXXI amoretti. Edmund Spenser.

Arthur Bliss was not a man to speak volubly of his deeper

emotions. He chose to let his music speak for him. This was the task Marguerite set herself whenever she played the piano music of Bliss. Her performance had to be such that her audience could 'hear' what the music had to say. On all her foreign tours the Bliss piano music was required.

There was a close understanding between composer and performer.

Shortly after the Portuguese tour Marguerite gave a recital at the Queen Elizabeth Hall in London.

In the first half of the programme she played the huge Chopin *Sonata in B minor, Opus 58,* and balanced this great work by including the equally huge Bliss *Piano Sonata* in the second half.

During this rehabilitation period in Marguerite's life, she and Dolly followed up their 'Lady Bliss' duet performance with several concerts. Their 'Four Hands - One Piano' programmes included such works as Mozart's *Sonata in D, K381,* Schubert's *Divertissement à la Hongroise, Opus 54,* and a big work by Schubert, the *Fantaisie in F minor, Opus 103.* This was a piece which particularly pleased and impressed Sir Arthur Bliss. He had already written a *Concerto for Two Pianos* (recorded by the Birmingham Symphony Orchestra with Cyril Smith and Phyllis Sellick as Soloists) and Sir Arthur said to Dolly that he

Roger, Angela, Dolly (Dorothy Wingate), Jonathan.

might consider writing something for four hands on one piano, and he thought he might use the title, *The Two Sisters*.

Marguerite and Dolly also played, of course, the very popular *Dolly, Opus 56* by Gabriel Fauré, with its distinctive sections; Berceuse, Le Jardin de Dolly, Kitty-Valse, Tendresse, and Le Pas Espagnol.

The sisters appeared professionally as 'Miss Marguerite Wolff and Miss Dorothy Wolff', but wife and mother-of-one Dolly became pregnant again and this, with the increasing demands on Marguerite's time, brought the partnership to a temporary halt.

(Dolly, who already had a daughter, Angela, gave birth to a son Roger. Less than three years later she had her third child, Jonathan.)

Marguerite's children, Crystal and Gloria, followed the same educational path during their early years, attending the same day school and, in addition, the Ballet Rambert school.

Crystal

As their personalities and tastes developed their schooling was chosen to fit their personal needs. Crystal wanted a career in films, so she went to Arts Educational, near Hyde Park Corner. This was conveniently situated because the family had left the large house in Avenue Road and was living in a smaller home in Park Lane. Gloria was developing academically, and she travelled each day to Camden School for Girls, before going on to university. She turned out to be a very fine scholar. Gloria is a very talented pianist but she has no ambition to go on to the concert platform. Having lived with all the hard work and dedication, and sometimes fear, of being a concert pianist, Gloria decided to simply enjoy her music.

The two sisters never had a feeling of 'Poor Mummy' after the loss of their father. Mother and the two daughters each had an independent life, a busy life, yet they remained a closely knit trio. Crystal was happy acting, and Gloria was happy reading Modern French, and gaining an M.A. in Ancient History, and later doing some research work at The Atheneum, Oxford, and, as we have seen, Marguerite was happy to be 'back home' on the concert platform.

Gloria was helped with her A-Level Music by George Berkovitz, who came to England as a refugee. He had been a pupil of Kodály for seven years, and he had known Bela Bartok. He was a frequent visitor to the family home and Marguerite had known him since she was thirteen. George had a great musical knowledge and, during one period, he spent countless hours going through the Wagner operas with Gloria. Right up to the time he died he remained a great friend of the family and his loss was much mourned.

Gloria

Referring to professional playing Marguerite said to Sir Arthur Bliss, 'It is a career yet it is not a career. It's so nebulous. You drift from one engagement to another.' Sir Arthur replied, 'Yes, indeed, it always amazes me when a concert actually comes off.'

But the concerts did come, both at home and overseas.

One of the 'home' concerts given by Marguerite was for a Reverend Raymond Walters who had started a Festival of Music, in Lincoln. For previous concerts the vicar had already engaged several top international artists, and these included (pre-war) Sergei Rachmaninoff, (post-war) Benno Moiseiwitsch, and Solomon. He had approached Marguerite during her marriage, asking her if she could find the time to support one of these Lincoln Festivals. This Marguerite now did, with Leon Goossens on the same programme. (As a matter of fact, the first concert Marguerite gave after Derrick's death was for the Reverend Walter's brother, in Shrewsbury.)

There was an amusing, if very uncomfortable, incident at the Shrewsbury concert. Marguerite was playing the Bliss *Sonata* (her first performance of it in England) and she was wearing a black velvet dress. While playing she was getting hotter and hotter and it was only afterwards that she discovered that the piano stool had been placed over a heating grill.

Marguerite attended a concert in Sheffield with Sir Arthur and Lady Bliss, and she went with them to the Cheltenham Festival, where *Morning Heroes* was performed. This work was for Sir Arthur's brother, Kennard, who was killed in 1916 in the Battle of the Somme. This symphony has five movements, and they describe war during all ages. The last movements ends with a poem *Dawn on the Somme,* by Robert Nichols, and it is sung by a chorus. Sir Arthur declares that his brother Kennard, being poet, painter and musician, was the most gifted member of the family. In 1920 Arthur Bliss revisited the battlefield where his brother fell, and in 1929 *Morning Heroes* was written, a work so vastly different in content from the *Serenade* for his wife, written the same year. These works reveal Bliss to be a man of great compassion, a man who retained the delicate edge to his finer feelings despite the influence World War One had in shattering cherished illusions and beliefs of those men who served in the trenches.

Sir Arthur Bliss, born in 1891, was educated at Rugby, and then he studied music at Cambridge and at the Royal College of Music. He enlisted in August, 1914, and the following year was sent to France as a captain. He took a portable gramophone into the trenches, his favourite records included music by Elgar,

Berlioz, and Schubert. Elgar and his wife had befriended Bliss in 1912 and had taken a great interest in his early career.

In 1916 Arthur Bliss was wounded, but later he joined the 1st Battalion of the Grenadier Guards and returned to France.

His Victory Medal bore oak leaves, to signify that he had been mentioned in despatches. During his war service he composed a piano quartet but, although it was published and performed, he was such a perfectionist he decided to withdraw the work.

After his demobilisation there was a steady stream of music from 1919 until 1939 when World War Two temporarily slowed his output. (1922 was probably the year when he was accepted as a major composer, following the success of his *Colour Symphony*.)

His patriotic background is, understandably, evident in much of his music, making him a superb choice as Master of the Queen's Musick, in 1953. He was knighted in 1950. Sir Arthur was keenly aware of great national events — Coronations, Royal Weddings, Investiture of a Prince of Wales — they meant much to him. When Churchill died Bliss's *March of Homage in Honour of a Great Man,* broadcast immediately before the funeral, showed the composer's noble pride in being strongly patriotic.

These were, of course, qualities dear to the heart of Marguerite and she was drawn close, not only to the music but also to Sir Arthur and Lady Bliss. They, in turn, welcomed Marguerite and became extremely fond of Crystal and Gloria.

When *The Musical Times* celebrated its 125th anniversary the editor invited Sir Arthur to write a commemorative piece. He wrote a clever *Miniature Scherzo,* dedicating it to Marguerite Wolff. Bliss founded his scherzo on a phrase from Mendelssohn's *Violin Concerto*, written in 1844, the year *The Musical Times* was first published.

To Marguerite Wolff

MINIATURE SCHERZO
for Piano

ARTHUR BLISS

(By kind permission of Lady Bliss and Novello and Co. Ltd.)

When Arthur Bliss' half-sister was getting married he asked her what she wanted for a wedding present and she said she would like him to compose a piece of music. He did this, and called the work *A Wedding Suite*. Then he rang Marguerite and asked her to record it. On the recording there is the voice of Arthur Bliss talking about his half-sister, then about the music, and then about the pianist, Marguerite Wolff. This spoken introduction is then followed by the actual performance of the piece. At the wedding this recording was played after the cake had been cut.

A Wedding Suite became part of Marguerite's extensive and varied repertoire and she played it on all tours; the Far East, Peru, Mexico, New York, and elsewhere.

It is very charming. The first movement is not unlike Scarlatti, and then there is a Fauré nocturne style creeping in. There is also a touch of the Blues idiom and it is quite jazzy in parts. It ends with a waltz. The piece goes down very well and its popularity has not diminished.

Ibbs and Tillett, as agents, arranged a concert at London's Queen Elizabeth Hall to celebrate the 80th birthday of Arthur Bliss. Marguerite was engaged to play his *Piano Sonata*. The Melos Ensemble played his marvellous *Clarinet Quintet (1931)*, with Gervase de Peyer as the soloist. Also on the programme was Bliss's wonderful song cycle, *Angels of the Mind (1969)*, a work which has a particularly beautiful piano accompaniment.

Late in his life he mentioned that he thought that Marguerite should take on his *Piano Concerto,* a work of great nobility. It had been commissioned by the British Council for the 1939 New York Fair, and the first performance took place there, the New York Philharmonic Orchestra being conducted by Adrian Boult, with Solomon as the soloist.

Arthur Bliss died in 1975 and in the memorial concert, *A Tribute to Sir Arthur Bliss,* arranged by Ibbs and Tillett, Marguerite was joined by fellow-artists, Thea King playing the *Clarinet Quintet* with the Melos Ensemble, and Peter Graeme playing the *Oboe Quintet* with the same ensemble.

When Arthur Bliss died it was an enormous blow to Marguerite. The loss of such a great musical figure, and one who had been such an influence in her life, was irreplaceable.

In return for his kindness Marguerite had done all she could to advance his music, and in his autobiography, *As I Remember,* (written before he knew Marguerite), he wrote in ink on the inside page of the book, 'For Marguerite, with gratitude for all she has done for my music, from, The Author.'

QUEEN ELIZABETH HALL

Director: JOHN DENISON, C.B.E.

Wednesday 30th June 1971
at 7.45 p.m.

Music by

ARTHUR BLISS

born 2nd August 1891

A Tribute by Friends in his 80th Year

MARGUERITE WOLFF *solo piano*
RAE WOODLAND *soprano*
LAMAR CROWSON *piano*
MEMBERS OF THE MELOS ENSEMBLE

Emanuel Hurwitz, violin Ivor McMahon, violin Cecil Aronowitz, viola
Terence Weil, cello Gervase de Peyer, clarinet

Piano Sonata (1952)
Song Cycle " Angels of the Mind " (1969)
Clarinet Quintet (1931)

Marguerite is not strictly a modernist, her taste being very much that of the classical Mozart, Schubert, and Beethoven, leading into the romantic period of Chopin, Mendelssohn and Liszt. Being a pupil of Kentner, who is President of the Liszt Society, and who Marguerite believes is probably the greatest exponent of Liszt in the world, it was natural for her to become a member of the Liszt Society. Eventually she became a member of the Council, and Council Meetings are held at her home.

96

Romano Cagnoni's photograph of Marguerite Wolff, Chandos House.

She made an interesting choice of Liszt's music on stereo record DF/1, Decca Record Company, the sleeve bearing the famous Ramano Cagnoni photograph of Marguerite at the piano. The recording has on Side One, *Magyar Dallok No. 12 in E minor,* a selection of Hungarian Rhapsodies by Liszt, followed by *Polonaise No. 1 in C minor,* which illustrates Liszt's interest in the music of his friend Chopin. Keith Fagan, writing on the record sleeve, says, 'the incredible closing bars seem to tell us that this is a Hungarian Polonaise. It is a work of great beauty, grandeur and majesty.'

On Side Two, Marguerite plays *Il Lamento (A flat major), La Leggierezza (F minor),* and *Un Sospiro (D flat major),* three studies which have been published under the title, *Trois Caprices Poétiques.* The third piece, *Un Sospiro,* is one of Liszt's most popular compositions. Referring to this piece Keith Fagan writes, 'It is interesting to note that towards the end of the piece Liszt, when playing it, used to insert a short passage of calm and serene chords before the final section. Miss Wolff plays this passage in this recording.'

Following a recital at The Queen Elizabeth Hall, London, Joan Chissell wrote in *The Times:*

'Marguerite Wolff divided her piano recital between Chopin and Liszt. She deserves particular gratitude for unearthing the *E flat minor Magyar Dallok (No. 12)* from the early set of nationalist pieces on which Liszt subsequently drew for his later Hungarian Rhapsodies. Miss Wolff did wonders in disentangling luscious themes from ornately embellished accompaniments. There was also much to enjoy in Liszt's three *Concert Studies of 1848,* particularly her excellent control in the final *Un Sospiro.'*

The *Daily Telegraph* wrote:

'The earlier part of the evening was devoted to Chopin for whom the recitalist proclaimed a special affection. The stylish performance of the four *Impromptus,* and the *A flat* and *G minor Ballades* were those of a pianist of real quality. This extremely cultivated pianist gave a spectacular performance of the Liszt *Fifth Hungarian Rhapsody,* which enthusiastically exploits the zymbalon effects.'

Marguerite had a wonderful concert with the London Symphony Orchestra (leader, her 'Brahms' conductor', George Stratton), conducted by John Foster, when she played the Liszt *Piano Concerto in E flat No. 1* Marguerite has, of course, played this concerto many times and with leading orchestras, notably with the Royal Philharmonic Orchestra at The Royal Festival Hall, London.

With the classical and romantic influence so strongly represented in Marguerite's music it was a most enriching experience for her to work so closely with a contemporary composer of the calibre of Sir Arthur Bliss.

It encouraged her, for example, to study *Three Short Dances* with the Portuguese composer himself, Fernando Lopes Graça, thus delighting the local audience during one of her Iberian tours. She introduced the same audience to Lovelock's *Etude and Scherzo,* and *Etude de Concert,* and also the Bliss *Miniature Scherzo.* Prominently featured in these recitals were Schumann's *Carnaval Opus 9,* Haydn's *F minor Variations,* and the Schubert *Impromptus,* surely a wonderful mixture of the classical, the romantic, and the contemporary. On many of these works Marguerite has given lecture-recitals.

Shortly after Arthur Bliss' death Marguerite was in New York at the start of one of her American tours. She had been asked to play the Bliss *A Wedding Suite.* It was the first performance of the work in America. The concert organisers played the cassette of Sir Arthur's voice introducing the work and Marguerite herself. She was taken totally unawares, and hearing Arthur Bliss's voice was a very eerie experience for her.

Marguerite's love for the music of Arthur Bliss had, like so many of the various loves in any person's life, come to her 'out of the blue'. It had begun at the time that Derrick died, but it did not end when Sir Arthur died, because Marguerite still is, and will remain so, a great exponent of the piano music of Sir Arthur Bliss, Master of the Queen's Musick, and Marguerite retains a great warmth, affection, and admiration for Lady Bliss, 'Trudy', Sir Arthur's widow.

Six

The majority of male concert pianists still wear the conventional white tie and tails and it is their female counterpart who display an individual choice of dress.

Marguerite, with her couturier, Wim Hemmink, enjoys planning a new concert dress.

Wim Hemmink, who on one occasion light-heartedly referred to Marguerite as his 'wolf in Wim's clothing', uses about thirteen metres of fabric for a concert dress. The design must allow plenty of room for the arms to cross over and for the pianist to move freely. He makes the dress slightly shorter in the front so that it is clear of the pedals, and he likes it to look elegant when she walks on to the platform. It is so designed that it falls into place over the stool when she sits at the piano.

The occasion must be considered when choosing what fabric to use. To quote an example, the marvellously painted hall in the Egyptian Room of The Mansion House, London, with its vivid turquoise and glorious colours, requires a careful choice of dress material to blend.

There are other concert situations to consider; an orchestral concert with the black and white of the orchestral players, the church concert, the memorial concert, the birthday concert and even, in Marguerite's case, the prison concert.

The dress should create a harmonious picture, be it with soloist and orchestra or the recital with just the stark black concert grand.

When preparing for a concert tour with probable changes of climate a varied wardrobe is necessary. Marguerite tries to have colours which blend with each other. For instance, for her trip to Peru the colour was yellow and everything else blended with the yellow mohair coat (a coat she was glad to wear when in the High Andes and the wonderful antiquity, Machu Picchu).

There can be great changes in temperature. One day there is the tremendous heat of, say, Calcutta followed a day or two later by the bitter cold of Darjeeling.

There was one concert in Jakarta, Indonesia, where the heat was so intense in an un-airconditioned hall that electric fans were tried. These blew Marguerite's hair all over her face and the dress billowed up, so the idea had to be abandoned. Marguerite played through the first half, and in the interval she felt rather

Lord Segal with Queen Elizabeth, the Queen Mother.

Lord and Lady Segal arranged for Marguerite Wolff to give a piano recital at The Mansion House, by kind permission of the Lord Mayor, Sir Anthony Jolliffe, G.B.E., D.Sc., in aid of the MENCAP City Foundation, June, 1983.

'. . . the marvellously painted hall in the Egyptian Room of The Mansion House, London, with its vivid turquoise and glorious colours, requires a careful choice of dress material to blend.'

like a boxer with 'her seconds' coming into the Artists' Room with a bowl of water and towels to cool her down. After the second half of the concert, followed by the Reception, Marguerite returned to her hotel, and the dress was so plastered to her it had to be torn off.

The Bliss Memorial Concert posed a problem. Some said black ought to be worn but others were against this. A compromise was found. A shimmering turquoise lamé was covered with filmy black lace, and this could not offend anyone's taste. Marguerite usually wears this dress when playing in places of worship.

Sometimes there are daytime concerts, so a short concert dress is part of her luggage in every overseas tour.

If Marguerite sees beautiful fabric, such as banana silk in the Philippines, Shantung in Taiwan, a gorgeous sari in India, she buys it to put away for the future.

In Bombay some marvellous fabric was embroidered in tiny pearl and diamonté flowers. This work took nine months and a friend of Marguerite's brought it to London where Wim Hemmink made it into a dress for a concert at the Royal Festival Hall.

Marguerite takes at least two concert dresses on tour; a zip might go, or there might be some other accident, or there could be a colour clash.

In Lusaka the concert was being held in the ballroom of the Intercontinental Hotel and a bright red carpet extended under the piano. Marguerite had a bright red concert dress with her and had she worn it, because it was the only one in her luggage, it would have been a disaster. Wisely she had a second dress, a more appropriate silver colour.

In Davao City, in the Philippines, Marguerite had a shower-bath contraption in her hotel room, but no bath. She wanted a large bowl of water, to sponge herself before putting on a beautiful chiffon and organza dress, which happened to be spread over the back of a chair. The oriental maid spoke no English so Marguerite used sign language and the maid signified that she understood. Some time later the polite little chamber-maid came to Marguerite, with great pride and a delightful sense of achievement shining in her face, and handed Marguerite the chiffon dress — dripping wet! Marguerite thanked her, wrapped the dress in a towel, and the girl never knew the dress was ruined.

At the Royal Festival Hall, London, after a performance of the Grieg *A Minor Piano Concerto* with The Royal Philharmonic Orchestra.

Duke of	Marguerite	Lady Buckley	Massino
Gloucester	Wolff		Freccia

Comments from the Far East:

'. . . Marguerite displayed elaborate evening affairs, classic day dresses, and a mohair cloak with a choice of two hemlines for colder climes.'

'. . . When she walks on to a platform, she likes the gown to follow behind her, it should fall nicely, covering the stool.'

'. . . She has Mr. Hemmink to design for her, and she has an enormous say in the creation. They shop together.'

A LITTLE NEARER HOME

Marguerite, Crystal and Gloria, holidaying in Venice.

Wherever she plays, home or abroad, Marguerite takes her piano stool. At airports this creates quite a stir.

She has sat on ammunition boxes in army camps, on stools that rocked whenever she moved, and there have been times when the only available chairs were two high and when the adjustable stool either jammed or would not wind down enough.

Violinists, cellists, trumpeters, and all the other numerous instrumentalists, can carry their own instruments. The days when concert pianists could travel with their own piano have long gone. The pianist, if he so wishes, can take his own stool and at least be able to sit comfortably. At one London school the music master noticed Marguerite having trouble with the school piano stool so he called to one of his boys, 'Open the hymn book at Psalm thirty-three and put it under the leg of the stool!'* Psalm thirty-three provided the correct thickness for Marguerite to have a firmly wedged stool for her recital.

We can thus understand why she goes to the trouble of travelling with a stool, despite the problems and incidents it sometimes creates.

At New York airport a man in a very loud check jacket and cap came up and said, looking at the stool, 'What'll ya take for it?'. Marguerite said, 'Sorry, not for sale!' and he persisted, 'Come on, now, I'll give you anything for it!'. She refused, and has regretted it ever since. It would have been simple to go into Steinways in New York, buy a new stool, and pocket a handsome profit!

It was on another visit to New York airport that she was met by her nephew, Charles Walford, and this bright young man improved the stool situation tremendously by presenting Marguerite with a set of detachable wheels. This was lovely for her. She felt she had gained her independence and no longer had to look for a big strong man to carry the stool for her.

She called the now-mobile stool, 'My Rolls!'

When her travels with a piano stool started, the Dorchester Hotel, her nearest neighbour, did an elaborate and elegant job in wrapping the stool. On arrival at Budapest airport this mysterious parcel caused so much suspicion at the Customs, and took so long to unwrap, that she has since always taken it in its naked state.

On Wings of Song

A GIBRALTAR incident in which Marguerite Wolff, the concert pianist, was involved last week shows that even politics may be frustrated by good nature.

After playing in Malaga, Miss Wolff took a Spanish car to La Linea after the frontier had been closed. So she tapped on the Customs office window and mimed piano playing.

Whereupon the Spanish officials came out, unloaded the car, secured a taxi, put her luggage and piano stool into it and waved her on to Gibraltar without asking to see her passport.

© *The Daily Telegraph.*

---

* Robert Leach has brought to my notice that Ps. 33 v.1. says 'praise befits the upright'! (R.C-L.)

Her Far East admirers were fascinated by Marguerite's antics with her piano stool.

'. . . She carried it with her while shuttling between Marco Polo Hotel and the Yamaha Music School where she has practised eight hours every day since she arrived here earlier this week.'

Marguerite's elegance also drew expressions of appreciation.

'. . . In a sky-blue dress that matched her sparkling blue eyes, lithe-looking Marguerite exudes elegance from every pore.'

One reporter who asked her age received this reply, 'I never mention my age as a point of principle.'

HAVE STOOL — WILL TRAVEL

To prison — with piano stool.

The pianist, having to play on whatever instrument is offered, likes to know the make of piano and this is usually his first question on arrival. Makes of piano can be good, bad, or indifferent as, for example, the different makes of motorcar.

Marguerite takes up the story of what frequently happens to the poor pianist.

'You arrive at the hall and you are shown the piano, and told, "Vladimir Ashkenazy thought it was all right!" and, "John Ogdon didn't complain!", and when you continue to look worried you are told, "We *are* having it tuned!", as though "having it tuned" will correct all defects in the mechanism!'

John Ogdon had an awful experience at a concert.

The orchestra was ready, so was the audience, and the conductor led the pianist on to the platform. Having bowed to acknowledge the applause he sat at the piano and tried to open the lid.

It was locked.

Eventually the man with the key was found in the boiler room, and the concert began a little late.

At concert halls in remote places it might have been months since the last concert took place, and since then the piano has remained locked and unplayed. A piano that is not used can be really dreadful.

It is rare to find terrible pianos in the big cities, but Marguerite did play at one London hall where the bass notes of the piano were sticking down.

'I was playing the *Waldstein*. The sonata starts with rapid notes, and there was someone sitting by the piano trying to push the notes up. It must have been very terrible.'

Sir Basil and Lady Lindsay-Fynn asked Marguerite to give a concert tour round Devon for the 'Preservation of Churches in Devon.' She was delighted to do this. Marguerite stayed in the beautiful home of the Lindsay-Fynns in Budleigh Salterton, and each day went to a different church, estate, or castle, to give a concert. She travelled by car, being driven by Mrs. Trudy Ruffle who safely navigated the unlit paths of Dartmoor.

One concert was in a beautiful castle, containing lovely antique furniture, and set in splendid grounds which included a waterfall. The piano, although unused, was not too bad.

The next concert was at a vast house which had about a hundred bedrooms, each unheated. There was a grand old lady living there, more or less in the kitchen and one bedroom. A girl from a farm came to help her. Marguerite takes up the story.

'The old lady was wearing a cardigan, and had her dogs with

her, when she met me at the door. We went into a wonderful library where the concert was to be held; it was circular. Then she showed me the piano. It was a Bechstein, and it had the signatures, Kaiser Wilhelm, and Princess Louise. It was beautifully signed by a long line of Royalty. It was, really, a rare and valuable antique. As an *objet d'art* it was beautiful, with sturdy bulbous legs. But everything else was fragile. The keys were yellow with age and, as I suspected, it had not been played for ages. The whole place was cold, the piano was cold, and it was still bitterly cold when the audience assembled. Pianists rarely complain about the pianos they have to play on, but this time I did announce that I was playing on a rather fragile, but charming, old lady, and I hoped she would survive.'

In Torquay there was a new church, on the top of a hill, and the designers had been very enterprising because when the building is not used as a church, a partition comes down in front of the altar, and the place becomes a concert hall. They had a modern Steinway piano on a modern stage. During the whole of the Devon tour this was the only decent piano she was given to play on.

Heat, such as in the tropics, can play havoc with pianos, with wood, steel strings and iron frame reacting differently to the high temperature. The glue holding the ivories can melt and it is not unknown for an inexperienced pianist to be disconcerted by the neat little rows of screws on the piano keys looking, in some cases, like bad fillings in teeth. Marguerite remembers a very old Steinway in Calcutta being treated in this way. At first encounter it can be a little distracting to the eye.

At another place, during one of her Far East tours, Marguerite had to give a recital on a romantic 'Roof Top Theatre'. It was necessary to lift the piano from the floor on to the platform and in doing this the men faltered and sliced off the entire mechanism of the pedals. Marguerite was standing there with the British Council representative, John Weston. There was a deadly silence and they looked at one another in horror. Mr. Weston called in a Chinese piano tuner who said he could achieve the impossible by putting the mechanism together again in time for the concert.

True to his word, with half an hour to go, he had the complete mechanism in working order. The audience arrived, and the recital began on time as if nothing untoward had happened.

Everyone is familiar with the single keyboard piano, few with the double-keyboard instrument developed by the brilliant Hungarian, Emanuel Moór. He was, possibly, a pupil of Liszt but he was certainly a Leonardo da Vinci type of all-round genius, being pianist, composer and inventor.

A succession of four rich wives had given him the means to indulge his inventive skills, and he had the idea of translating the ancient two-keyboard harpsichord into a modern two-keyboard piano.

His fourth wife, Winifred Christie, a pupil of Harold Bauer, was not only wealthy but was also a great concert pianist. She gave concerts all over the world on the Bösendorfer-Moór* double-keyboard piano. She chose Marguerite, who was about seventeen at the time, to study this double-keyboard instrument. Miss Christie was not living in England but paid regular visits and stayed for a week or so at a time. She gave Marguerite a two hour lesson every day, at the Trudy Huttenbach studio in St. John's Wood. The piano was very large and, being purpose-made, was very expensive.

It was possible to play the Schubert duos with two hands, and it was ideal for works like the Bach *D minor Toccata and Fugue*.

There was an octave coupler, a third pedal, and the upper keyboard was one octave higher than the lower keyboard. The invention was intended to be a development of the piano.

It might have been more successful if Miss Christie had engaged young composers to write for this instrument rather than use pianists to learn adaptations of music already successfully performed on the single-keyboard piano.

Less and less was heard of this piano and, inevitably, Marguerite's interest waned.

Several years went by when 'out of the blue' Miss Christie contacted Marguerite and suggested meeting at the Central Music Library, Victoria.

Marguerite remembers this meeting.

'I went in and saw a fragile-looking lady sitting in front of a typewriter. She looked up and said, "Just a minute", and went on typing. Then she got up and kissed me. Looking round the library she said, "Isn't this all wonderful!", and I agreed.

'For the last year she had spent her time and money developing the marvellous, and in some ways unique, library.

'She took me to the Victoria Coach Station for lunch and said I must have Bovril in milk and a cheese sandwich. I was still so in awe of her I drank and ate it up.

'Her purpose in meeting me was to ask if I would house and play again her Bösendorfer-Moór piano.

'I said I would think about it and let her know. Alas, I should have said "Yes" right away. A few days later I telephoned, to be told she had died the day before.'

* According to Oxford Companion the instruments were built by Blüthner.

It is to the orthodox single-keyboard piano that Marguerite has spent her life. Shakespeare, on watching a girl's fingers playing the keys of the early keyboard instrument, the virginal, created the now well-worn phrase, 'tickle the ivories',

To be so tickled, they would change their state
And the situation with those dancing chips,
O'er whom thy fingers walk with gentle gait
Making dead wood more blest than living lips.

Pianists invariably have a preference for whose 'dancing chips their fingers walk o'er with gentle gait'. Mozart, who as a child saw the world because he was a travelling pianist, preferred the pianos made by the father of one of his pupils. In 1711 he wrote, 'I much prefer Stein's pianofortes, for they damp ever so much better than . . .' and he named one or two others. When Beethoven began to smash pianos it was realised that the fault lay in the piano and not in Beethoven's music. Great strides were then made in the development of the piano and the names of the leading makers became famous, Bechstein, Bösendorfer, Pleyel, Clementi, Steinway, Blüthner, Broadwood, Erard, to mention but a few, and the piano gained not only in strength but also in size, growing from the four octaves of Cristofori's primitive piano to the present keyboard of seven and a quarter octaves (88 notes).

Marguerite prefers the Steinway.

Her parents originally had a Bechstein but they changed it for an old Steinway and Marguerite and Dolly found that it suited them admirably.

Their nanny, Alice Percival, loved her two little charges (when Dolly was born she called her 'my little woman') and when Alice died her will confirmed this love. Throughout her service with Nina and Walter she had saved all her wages. During that time she refused to take holidays or spend money on herself. She left it all to Marguerite and to Dolly.

Marguerite decided to buy a new Steinway and when the manager of the London branch of Steinways came to the house and saw how well the seventy year old piano had stood up to the test of time he exclaimed, 'It makes you proud!'

Steinways are renowned for the pride they take, not only in the making of their instruments but also in the continuing welfare of 'their' concert artists who own Steinway pianos.

The piano went to her first home when she married, and then to Avenue Road. When it needed to be reconditioned Marguerite took Steinway's advice and bought a new and slightly larger grand piano.

Statue of Mozart.

Bronze violinist in the hallway of Marguerite's home, Chandos House.

A corner of Marguerite's lounge, Chandos House.

Robert Glazebrook, now General Manager of Steinways, London, advised Marguerite that the time had come to change her piano. She had moved into Park Lane, and it was advice she was pleased to accept.

A similar change of pianos took place when Marguerite moved to Chandos House in Belgravia. Robert Glazebrook met her one morning, they flew to Hamburg, narrowed the choice of pianos at the Steinway factory down to six and because the choice was so difficult, Marguerite turned to Mr. Glazebrook and said, 'You choose one for me!'

This he did. They flew back to London and the whole operation had taken place in one day. Some weeks later a beautiful piano was delivered to Chandos House.

When Marguerite plays abroad, Steinways in London contact their overseas representatives and wherever possible a Steinway piano is provided for Marguerite's concerts. Robert Glazebrook has given several television interviews explaining the relationship his company likes to maintain with the concert artist.

Steinways are, of course, prominent in New York, and have played a big part in co-operating with Marguerite during her American tours.

In the case of Steinways, the family moved from the Harz mountains of Central Germany to New York in 1850, forming *Steinway and Sons* in 1853 and opening their first New York factory in the following year. Many families left Europe and settled in America during the 19th and 20th centuries, and one of these was the musical Kurtz family, who became friends of Marguerite's.

A 'long-lost cousin' of Derrick's who lived in Finland was compiling a family tree. This was Sidney Scott, and he visited Derrick and Marguerite in London. Later, when he learnt that Marguerite was going to New York he told her that he was a good friend of the Kurtz family and arranged an introduction.

She met the family, and has remained friends since.

Marguerite had, of course, heard of them. Efrem Kurtz, the famous conductor, Arved, the violinist and composer, Edmund the cellist, and their violinist sister, Mary Rosenwald, and she says, 'To be with the Kurtz family really is an experience. They are all extraordinarily amusing, very vivacious, and they drift from one language to another. Arved has a very sweet wife, Susie, who is a writer. They have all been refugees twice, first from Russia, then from Germany to America.'

Marguerite has given many concerts in New York, some of the early ones being arranged by His Excellency, Ivor Richards, Q.C., U.K. Permanent Representative to the United Nations, and two were arranged by John Walsh, Deputy Consul General in New York at the time.

Beneficiaries from Charity Concerts were The Daughters of The British Empire, and also Trinity College of Music, when a Trust Fund was set up to celibrate their Centenary. The Principal at the time, Myers Foggin, presented a gold medal to Vladimir Horowitz.

At one of Marguerite's visits to America she gave the world premiere of the Bliss *A Wedding Suite* at the Town Hall, New York. This was a concert of British music and Arved Kurtz, with some of his assistants from the Juilliard School, performed works by Frank Bridge and Edward Elgar. John Walsh, with the support of his wife, arranged this concert. In a letter to Dr. Myers Foggin, the Principal, John Walsh places the credit where it is due, 'The main promoter of the event was, of course, Arved Kurtz, who freely gave of his time and enthusiasm.'

Arved Kurtz

John Walsh took Marguerite to see the wonderful Steinway factory in Queens, and to meet Mr. John Steinway.

Of the concert John Walsh writes,

'The principal recital was the performance of the first public playing of *A Wedding Suite* by Sir Arthur Bliss. The concert was in the Town Hall, New York, and was in aid of two charities, The Daughters of the British Empire, and Trinity College of Music, London. A quintet of players from the Julliard School of Music, New York, was led by Dr. Arved Kurtz.

I also arranged for Marguerite to give a recital at Ramapo College, Northern New Jersey, which took place on the 15th — the Ides of March! All went well.'

Practice is ever a problem on tour, but organisers are always sympathetic, anywhere in the world, as these letters indicate—

From the British Embassy in Athens, Michael Stewart wrote,

'Don't worry about being a nuisance when you are practising. There is quite a good Steinway in the house and nothing gives me greater pleasure than to be around when somebody is practising.'

And from the British Embassy in Lisbon, Sir Anthony Lambert wrote,

'. . . the drawing room in which the piano is, will be entirely free for your use. Far from objecting to hearing a pianist practising we rather like it.'

Steinways were particularly helpful in New York, and Marguerite is extremely appreciative of this service.

Mr. Charles Dalldorf and his wife entertained Marguerite on the top floor of the World Trades Building; the view presented is rather like seeing New York from the air. John Walsh writes of a typical example of American enthusiasm,

'Mrs. Dalldorf was so thrilled to have a famous pianist as her guest that in a not untypical American way, she insisted that poor Marguerite should play on the grand piano in the restaurant.'

Marguerite played Chopin's *Minute Waltz* — and the knives and forks stopped clattering as the music flowed from 'the highest piano in the world!'

Her American visits were full of incident — for example, being held up in a traffic jam and arriving for a broadcast with only one minute to spare — but space does not permit a fuller account.

Another exciting dimension was added to Marguerite's musical life when she joined the Liszt Society and Louis Kentner, President, invited her to join the Council of Management. The

World famed pianist LOUIS KENTNER is shown at a new Steinway on the occasion of a Liszt Society concert in the London home of Marguerite Wolff. Long associated with the music of Liszt, Louis Kentner has said of the Steinway, 'The Steinway piano is, for me, more than an instrument; it is an inspiration and a life-long friend.'

Society publishes an excellent journal, the editor being Adrian Williams.

For her first meeting with the council she invited them to her home and thus began a series of meetings, at six-week intervals, which hostess Marguerite found enchanting. The members were so illustrious she felt that she was part of Schumann's *Davidsbündler*. It was sometimes difficult for the Chairman to keep order, there were so many people with important things to say.

The Liszt Society has a world-wide membership and is supported by subscriptions and donations. Contacts are maintained with Liszt Societies in Hungary, U.S.A., France, Italy, Netherlands, Australia and Czechoslovakia. The Society Journal is a scholarly work.

The President of the Society is Mr. Louis Kentner, C.B.E., who provided a highlight in 1984 activities by playing in the Assembly House, Norwich. Liszt himself played there in 1840. Alan Paul is the Society's organiser, and the activities include recitals, competitions, visits, and encouragement to young artists. 1986 will be the centenary of Liszt's death and this will be suitably honoured.

114

The A.G.M.'s are held at the home of Marguerite Wolff. At the conclusion of the business, Louis Kentner gives a piano recital, and this is followed by Marguerite's staff serving a buffet supper to the 80 or 90 members present.

*This company of music-lovers is very near to Marguerite's heart.

* Officers, Patrons, and Council of Management: Louis Kentner, C.B.E., Sir Sacheverell Sitwell, Bart., C.H., Dr. Vernon Harrison, Christopher Srawley, Eunice Mistarz, Vladimir Ashkenazy, Alfred Brendel, France Clidat, Gunnar Johansen, The Lord Londonderry, Yehudi Menuhin, K.B.E., Lord Rayne, Sir Georg Solti, K.B.E., Robert Collet, Frank Daunton, Paul Gregory Mrs. L. Kustow, Mrs. Crystal Macnab, Paul Merrick, Alan Paul, Kenneth Souter, Adrian Williams, Marguerite Wolff.

Seven

The careful organising which has gone into the planning of Marguerite's overseas tours, the contacts and friendships built up over many years, and the sheer experience of travelling, have combined to create for Marguerite the professional expertise and smooth efficiency which characterizes her globe-trotting today.

Travel can bring immense pleasure. It can educate, or, as Francis Bacon in his *Essays* writes,

'Travel, in the younger sort, is a part of education; in the elder, a part of experience.'

The experience, however, can sometimes cause concern. Four recent concert tours; to Mexico, Peru, Central Africa, and the Far East, involved incidents of international significance and there was a certain amount of worry among Marguerite's family in England because, in turn, earthquake, war hysteria, kidnapping and assassination were making news headlines from the very place where the family's travelling pianiste happened to be.

Mexico was a country Marguerite had long wanted to visit so she was particularly delighted as she made preparations for this concert tour.

When a friend, Sir John Buckley, Chairman of Davy International, heard of the trip he arranged for Marguerite to stay at a magnificent hotel which was more or less reserved for special guests, and when Steinways heard, they sent a piano to the suite reserved for her. Sir John also asked his friend Sir John Galsworthy (a direct descendant of the writer of *The Forsyte Saga*) and Lady Galsworthy to 'look after' Marguerite.

She gave three concerts in Mexico City; first a Chopin-Liszt programme which the Mexican Broadcasting Company recorded live. It was planned to go out in ten days' time, so Marguerite would still be in Mexico and could hear it if she wished. The second concert in the city was at the Instituto Anglo-Mexicano de Cultura, to a mixed Mexican and British audience, and the third was a glamorous concert for the British Ambassador, where all the cultural organisations in the city were represented. The concert was followed by a splendid dinner.

Although Marguerite's itinerary was heavy there was one free day when Lady Galsworthy was able to show Marguerite the wonders, and the spell, of Mexico.

Mexico City itself is highly-strung, eclectic, and so varied that the visitor can form no opinion as to what is typical 'Mexican'. Is it the sitting figure, hat over eyes, taking a prolonged siesta? Or is it the industrious *cargador* who has carried a hundred-pound load on his back over forty miles of mountain roads?

Marguerite was taken to the lava-bed area known as the Pedregal, and to the Cuicuilco pyramid, and also to the excavations revealing the secrets and treasures of the ancient Aztecs.

There is the gleaming modern *Centro Médico,* with its research centres, laboratories, hospitals and doctors, to whom wage-earning Mexicans can go for free treatment — and a few streets away is the *curandera,* who will cure by rubbing egg on the patient's body, or by prescribing nasturtium leaves, or rosemary, or even an amulet to guarantee love.

Lady Galsworthy's explanations to Marguerite were so colourfully informative that soon a group of tourists joined on to learn more of the secrets of this land 'south of the border'.

After lunch Marguerite and her distinguished guide went shopping in the open market where, Marguerite confesses, 'I spent far too much!'.

Mexico was so gloriously unpredictable and inexplicable that one could almost forgive the Mexican Press for writing 'Arthur Bills', instead of 'Arthur Bliss'.

The evening of the broadcast arrived, and the hotel tuned the set in Marguerite's room ready for the 9.00 p.m. relay. Exactly at 9.00 p.m. the set stopped working, the lights went out, and the room started shaking and swaying.

Marguerite was furious at this distressingly-timed interference, and staggering into the wobbling corridor she saw a man and she called out, 'My radio set has gone off!' and the man called back, 'Yes. We're in the middle of an earthquake!' Noticing Marguerite's sudden realisation of the real cause of the break-down in transmission he called out, 'Don't worry. It's a vertical earthquake. Not as bad as a horizontal one!'

Vertical or Horizontal, it was a big earthquake, widely reported in the English newspapers, so Marguerite's family were very concerned.

The Chopin-Liszt broadcast went out some weeks later, but by then Marguerite was safely back in England. Lady Galsworthy heard the broadcast and wrote to say that it sounded excellent.

Who can say what caused that earthquake at exactly nine o' clock that evening!

The tour of Peru was the last one of Marguerite's to be handled by Wilfred Van Wyck. There were two concerts in Lima; and the other places where Marguerite played included Arequepa and Torjillo. Her tour was sponsored by the Banco Nor Peru Continorte and was under the auspices of The British Council. It was August, 1983 and, because of the Falklands War, the tour had been on and off. In Peru feelings about the England-Argentine conflict still ran high and when it became known that the Bank of Peru was sponsoring a British artiste there were protest marches and the possibility of ugly scenes.

However, Marguerite did not know that she was the object of noisy protest. Her hosts kept her well protected and her performance was not under the emotional stress it might have been had she been aware of this public hostility.

The Lima concert, at the Casa de la Emancipacion, was in one of the most beautiful settings Marguerite has ever played in. The recital was televised, and this, too, inadvertently protected Marguerite because although the heat of the lights attracted all sorts of insects, and she claims to be 'terrified' of these creatures, the noise of the television cameras drowned the buzzing of the creatures' wings, so she was not aware of their unwelcome presence.

If we may diverse just for a moment Marguerite tells another 'insect story', one which took place in Calcutta several years before the Peruvian tour. During a recital an extremely large cockroach appeared on the front of the stage and, in full view of the audience, made its stately way towards the piano until it reached the tip of Marguerite's dress. The audience held its breath. Fortunately the cockroach was not a lover of classical music, so it turned round and slowly crawled off stage, the audience audibly heaving a sigh of relief. An artist grows to expect a certain audience-reaction and it can be worrying if this does not fulfil expectations. The peculiar audience-reaction was explained to Marguerite afterwards — and one is left to ponder; do cockroaches have tastes in music? Now, if Marguerite had been playing *La Cucaracha!*

But, to return to Peru. The televised recital was so well received that any post-Falklands feelings were forgotten, and Marguerite was left to enjoy the beauties of the country; a particular excitement for her being a trip to the High Andes.

Her Press reports were excellent.

Earlier in this book we mentioned that the Spanish say, 'I touch the piano', rather than 'I play the piano', and it makes charming reading when Peruvian reporter, Karyna de Orbegoso, writes,

'. . . La pianista inglesa que en esta oportunidad nos deleitara con el piano HA TOCADO (Caps. Mine R. C-L.) con las más famosas orquestas de

118

Londres, de Europa y de Estados Unidos.' . . . she, '*has touched* the piano with the most famous orchestras of London, Europe, and The United States.'

Although Wilfred was not alive to arrange the 1984 tour to Central Africa, Marguerite's path there was so well-worn from previous visits that she planned everything with the supreme efficiency born of experience.

Marguerite slept on the British Airways flight to Nairobi so that when the plane landed at 5.45 a.m. she was rested. Old friends, Nat and Cynthia Kosky, met her at the airport and took her to where she was staying, the famous 'Mount Kenya Safari Club.' (It is the epitome of luxury, with a very exclusive membership. The manager, Mr. Snelling, had given Marguerite a wonderful suite). The full poster for her first concert read:—

KENYA NATIONAL THEATRE

Sunday, July 8th, 1984 at 6.30 p.m.

KENYA CONSERVATOIRE OF MUSIC

presents

MARGUERITE WOLFF
(of the Liszt Society)

'. . . this extremely cultivated Pianist, a pianist of real quality.' *Daily Telegraph.*

Music by: Beethoven, Brahms, Chopin, Mendelssohn and Schubert.

Sponsored by

MOUNT KENYA SAFARI CLUB.

Marguerite is full of praise and admiration for the manner in which Nat Kofsky built up the excellent Kenya Conservatoire of Music.

Nat was born in London, son of a Latvian musician, John Kofsky, who was a naturalised Englishman. During World War Two Nat served with the British Forces in Nairobi. In 1957 he became Director of the Conservatoire and, without State aid, built up the standard of music to the highest order. For this work he was awarded the O.B.E. by the British Government, and the Polish Government awarded him the Karol Szymanowski Medal. He also has honorary membership of the Royal College of Music, London. He retired in 1984, but retained full interest in visiting artists.

Nat Kofsky arranged for Marguerite to practice all day at the Conservatoire. She had, of course, her own stool and she 'camped out' for the day relying for sustenance on a thermos flask of coffee and several bags of Sunmaid Raisins, supplemented by an apple.

Nat Kofsky

LAST Wednesday mark
the end of an era in
history of music in Nairo
It is when the widely admir
Nat Kofsky, violinist, c
ductor, music commenta
and broadcaster retired
Director of Kenya's Cons
vatoire of Music, a respo
bility which he had held a
both faithfully and imag
tively discharged for
years.

(By kind permission).

She had slept overnight and here she was in Africa practising all day, with not a minute lost. That evening she had dinner with Nat Kofsky and Cynthia, who was born on an African farm and, Elsa-like, reared three lion cubs. Cynthia is a most remarkable lady and is described by Journalist Edward Rodwell in this manner;

'Cynthia, who I know well, is artistic in every sense: music, lyrics, poems, illustrations.'

In 1956 she wrote *Kenya, Land of the Lion* for the first Kenya Olympic team, and from the countless songs she has written over a period of fifty years is the strangely haunting *Thorn Trees,* a favourite of Roger Whittaker.

Nat says, 'I plan a quiet life for Cynthia and myself,' but not so quiet that he cannot entertain and make arrangements for visiting friends such as Marguerite Wolff.

120

For her concert in the main theatre there was a problem because it was being used in the daytime so practice on the stage was not possible. The Blüthner concert grand, however, was kept 'locked away', and Marguerite was led to a shed-like box within which was the treasured piano. It was politely put to her that if she would like to practise with the piano in its 'box' she could do so. And this she did, rather like singing in the bathroom, and piano and artist arrived safely on stage in time for the evening concert, practice having been completed. Next day she had a broadcast, and then it was 'into the jungle', with posters on the trees, and the sound of animals for accompaniment. Thanks to weekly broadcasts by Nat Kofsky, the audiences understood the music Marguerite played, and it was, overall, a thrilling experience to witness the appreciation of different cultures.

Marguerite's next venue was Zambia, and there was a moment of fear for Marguerite when the huge customs official refused to let her pass at the airport. Then a grin spread across his face. He had heard Marguerite play and decided to play his little joke on her. The hospitality en route was very good, and soon the plane landed at Lusaka airport.

There were posters, 'Stamp Out Corruption', and during her stay Marguerite came to the conclusion that the President was working hard for his country, but it was sad to see famine, and large burnt-up areas of land.

She was met by Richard Timms, British Council representatives in Zambia, and at his home she met Richard's charming Norwegian wife. After dinner they told Marguerite about a miraculous escape from the jaws of a crocodile which their youngest son, Eirik, had made. The family were on safari holiday on the border of Zimbabwee and suddenly the elder son screamed 'Crocodile!'. A crocodile had Eirik's leg in its mouth and was dragging him under the water to drown him. Eirik kept punching at the croc's eyes and the beast loosened its jaws momentarily. In that split second Eirik jerked himself free. His leg was in ribbons, and there was a large hole in his hand. They rushed him to a nearby clinic for an anti-tetenus injection, and a big injection of valium, and then there was a one hundred mile dash to the nearest hospital. Eirik survived and later told his English Boarding School Headmaster, 'If you get caught by a croc., punch it in the eye!'

Such an escape was unheard of, and Eirik was young enough to recover the use of his leg and hand.

Fortunately there were no crocodiles near the Intercontinental Hotel where, in the magnificent ballroom, Marguerite gave a concert for the distinguished Lusaka Musical Society. She played the Beethoven *Sonata in C, opus 53 (Waldstein)*, and music by Schubert, Brahms, Mendelssohn and Chopin. The piano happened to be a very fine Steinway concert grand and this pleased Marguerite. She played a piece she discovered, she forgets where, and it is one she has not heard played anywhere. The audience loved its beautifully evocative lilt. This was a piece by Mendelssohn, *Gondollied*.

The next day Marguerite met the young crocodile hero, Eirik Timms, and his brother and very pretty sister were also present.

Schoolboy escapes 'croc'

AN ASHTEAD schoolboy has returned from a holiday in Africa he is never likely to forget.

In fact, 13-year-old Eirik Timms, a boarder at City of London Freemen's School, is lucky he came back at all.

For he nearly became one of the 40 people killed each year by crocodiles.

He had severe leg and arm injuries after he was attacked near a holiday chalet rented by his parents near Victoria Falls, in Zimbabwe.

One evening the two brothers decided to go fishing in a small inlet which bordered the grounds. Eirik set off on his own across a log to the other bank of the inlet to find a good spot.

It was starting to get dark, the water was still and he suspected nothing as he crossed the log. But when he got to the other side he heard what he thought was a hippopotamus and turned

Eirik Timms: a lucky escape.

back. Then a crocodile seized his leg.

For the next 45 seconds he fought for his life. The crocodile was trying to tear his leg off and when he tried to hit it with his hand it grabbed that as well.

His horrified brother could only watch as he was pulled under the water.

Eirik said: 'He kept pulling me down and trying to twist my

arm and I was thinking this just cannot be happening to me.'

Miraculously he was able to scramble free. Somehow he managed to get up the bank and into the arms of his father, who had come running when he heard the screams.

His father took him to the township at Victoria Falls but the clinic did not have the facilities to treat him.

They had to drive more than 65 miles to another hospital. Eirik was on a drip for a week and in hospital another two.

He returned to school bearing the scars on his leg and arms which he willingly shows to fellow pupils.

'My mum says something like that could only happen to a person once,' says Eirik cheerfully.

His advice to his friends is, 'If ever you are attacked by a crocodile poke it in the eyes!'

(By kind permission).

Marguerite at Livingstone Statue, Victoria Falls, with Horatio (river) and Athe Ellerup (Danish engineer), 1984.

There was a broadcast next day, recorded for future use, and for this Marguerite played a predominantly Liszt programme.

Then Marguerite paid an eagerly awaited visit to Victoria Falls, the Statue of Livingstone, and, upstream from the Falls, a short distance from the river, a large baobab known as 'The Big Tree', beneath whose massive branches the early pioneers made their camps. The name of her jungle driver was 'Sylvester', which reminded her that her driver's name in Peru was, inappropriately, 'Reliable'.

The African tour lasted for two and a half crowded weeks and the flight home was via Nigeria. Here the plane was infuriatingly held up for a long time. Of course, Marguerite knew nothing of the Dikko kidnap scandal, when this deposed Nigerian millionaire and former Transport Minister of the Lagos Government, was drugged, put into a diplomatic crate, taken to Stanstead airport, and almost smuggled out of England to face investigation in Nigeria. There were arrests in England, and no-one was certain what would happen to Marguerite and the other passengers temporarily stranded in Nigeria.

Fortunately the plane was allowed to leave and it arrived at Gatwick a little late. Marguerite had less than two full days to arrange a soirée at her home, for eighty people.

These adventures in far-flung countries do not diminish in any way the excitement of playing in Europe. Marguerite remembers with awe her first appearance at the Liszt Academy in Budapest, and remembering the long line of haloed pianists who had played there. If one has any imagination one can 'feel' the atmosphere, one can appreciate that Liszt, Bartok, Kodaly — musicians of that calibre, had played there. Marguerite says, 'No hall in the world has thrilled me more.'

An advantage which Europe and America has over some other, and possibly more romantic, parts of the world is the availability of symphony orchestras with which a concert pianist can perform piano concertos. Marguerite's repertoire of concertos includes:— Liszt *No. 1 in E flat*, Brahms *No. 1 in D minor*, Bach *F minor*, Beethoven *No. 1 in C major* and *No. 3 in C minor*, Schumann *A minor*, Grieg *A minor*, Tschaikovsky *No. 1 in B flat*, Bliss *Piano Concerto*, Mozart *Concerto in E flat* (two pianos), and, of course, a vast range of works for piano and orchestra, like Alec Rowley's *Ballet Suite for Piano and Orchestra* (dedicated to Marguerite Wolff). Then there is so much chamber music which she enjoys playing, such as

123

Marguerite plays to a packed Royal Albert Hall.

Schumann *Duos*, Beethoven and Haydn *Trios*, Mozart, Brahms, Schumann *Quartets*, Brahms and César Franck *Quintets*, Saint-Saëns *Septet,* and the glorious Violin and Piano Sonatas by, in particular, Beethoven and Brahms.

Marguerite did have one more overseas tour planned for 1984, a flight halfway round the world to the Philippines, with a series of concerts in India on the way back to England.

But first of all there was an important concert to prepare for at The Royal Albert Hall, London.

This was 'The Malcolm Sargent Summer Concert' in aid of his Cancer Fund for Children. The Royal Patron of this fund is Her Royal Highness The Princess of Wales, but she was unable to attend because of the birth of her second son, Prince Henry Charles Albert David, 15th September, 1984. Marguerite's concert was on the 16th.

Prince Harry was not the only baby to be born during the summer of 1984. On June 1st Marguerite's eldest daughter, Crystal, gave birth to a daughter, Ondine.

In the family tradition Crystal continued her acting career until after the seventh month of pregnancy.

I, the author, during a visit to the Park Lane flat where Crystal lives with Richard, her husband, can testify that Ondine is fit, lively, and beautiful, having successfully nursed her while Crystal read parts of the typescript.

Crystal

Marguerite had an ideal programme for a concert billed as a *Viennese Evening,* with The Wren Orchestra of London, conducted by Vilem Tausky, and a choir of 500 voices.

In the first half she played Mozart's *Rondo in F major (K 459),* for piano and orchestra. This work fitted beautifully into the Viennese programme.

In the second half she played *Soirée de Vienne No. 6* (for piano and orchestra), by Liszt, based on the waltzes of Schubert, and orchestrated by Tausky. Liszt wrote nine Soirées de Vienne, all based on Schubert's music.

One critic wrote,

'. . . Marguerite was an ideal interpreter of both the works she performed last night, as was made clear by the audience's warm and enthusiastic reaction to her playing. In addition to this Marguerite has a personal charisma, and her charm, dignity, poise and radiance won the hearts of the huge Albert Hall audience as much as the beauty and brilliance of her playing.'

K. Fagan.

英國著名鋼琴家瑪格麗特·吳
前日於已關吳，會奏演琴鋼場一行
（社央中）。北臺連抵英由

There was little time to bask in the success of this London concert because plans had to be made for a Far East tour.

Marguerite had plenty of experience, with at least seven tours to the Orient behind her. Taiwan (playing Yamaha pianos), Singapore, Calcutta, Indonesia, Bangkok, Malaysia, Sarawak, Borneo, Napal (flight to Mount Everest), Penang, Delhi, Manila, Katmandu — she was no stranger to these distant places.

Nor was she unused to the hectic travel arrangements necessary for the fulfillment of her concert itinerary. Consider her 1981 Far East flight details:—

Saturday	4th April	London/Delhi
Sunday	5th April	Delhi/Khartoum
Sunday	12th April	Khartoum/Bangkok
Monday	13th April	Bangkok/Jakarta
Tuesday	21st April	Jakarta/Kuala Lumpur
Saturday	25th April	Kuala Lumpur/Penang
Sunday	26th April	Penang/Kuala Lumpur
Sunday	26th April	Kuala Lumpur/Kuching
Sunday	26th April	Kuching/Sibu

(N.B. Three flights in one day, R.C-L.)

Wednesday	29th April	Sibu/Kuching
Thursday	30th April	Kuching/Singapore
Friday	1st May	Singapore/London

(arriving 08.30, Saturday, 2nd May).

Marguerite Wolff with the British Ambassador and Mrs. Tripp (Bangkok).

Even news of murder and devastating typhoons in the Philippines did not deter Marguerite. General Fabian Ver, top military adviser to President Marcos, was indicted (5th November, 1984) on charges of double murder following the 1983 assassination of the opposition leader, Benigno Aquino. On the same day Typhoon Agnes struck the central Philippines. Agnes was the 18th major storm to hit the Philippines that year, bringing the death total to over one thousand.

Marguerite finalised her tour arrangements and, complete with piano stool, arrived in Manila . . . only to be told that Mrs. Gandhi had been assassinated!

Despite this shocking news Marguerite was encouraged to keep to her concert schedule.

127

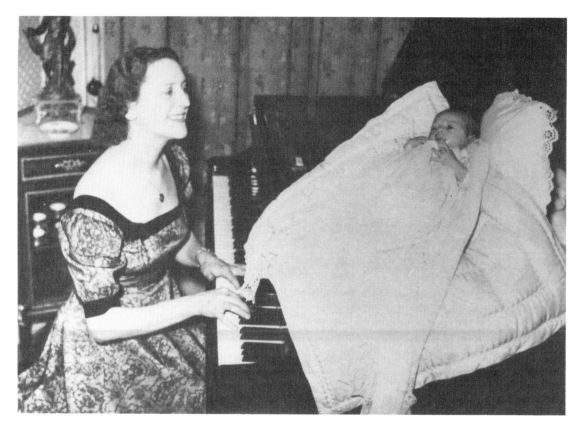

Marguerite and her daughter Crystal.

During her Far East tour of 1984 Marguerite's thoughts would have been with her eldest daughter, Crystal, who now had a daughter of her own, 5-month-old Ondine.

Her visits to other towns were sometimes delayed *en route* because of the damage caused by the typhoon. Madame Marcos, wife of the President, was active in visiting some of the worst hit areas and in urging speedy restoration work.

At one place, overlooking the blue sea, university girls appeared and in a scene which would have done credit to *South Pacific* they placed a necklace of shells on Marguerite. All was perfect until Marguerite met the piano. It looked odd, the inside felts were out of place, and even the inscrutible smile of the Oriental piano tuner could not hide from the most tone-deaf of hearers that the piano was impossibly out of tune. The locals were very proud of this piano; it was Manila-made but to disguise its origin it had been given a German-sounding name, *Wicbritstein*, a name which also looked slightly Victorian British! It transpired that a local musician, a professional, had selected it. 'A pianist?' Marguerite asked. 'Ah, no!' was the reply, 'a flute player!'

Andrew Kyle, British Council Representative, stood over the piano tuner for more than four hours. Miraculously, it did not sound too bad at the evening concert. Marguerite, to her credit, kept to her policy of never complaining about the piano.

There were excavations going on in the area and a lot of Ming pottery was being brought up from some very old Chinese graves, and Marguerite bought a beautiful Ming vase for her daughter, Gloria.

Back in Manila there were telephone calls from Marguerite's nephew, solicitor Martin Walford, who looks after her legal and managerial affairs. There were reports of riots in India, with thousands being killed. It seemed sensible to cancel Marguerite's tour of India, following the assassination, the rioting, and the existing state of mourning, so notices were sent there. Her air tickets were all changed so that she could return to London when her Philippines tour was completed.

She gave a lecture-recital on November 12th to the pupils of *La Salle Green Hills* High School, where the Catholic Principal, Brother Gus, presented Marguerite with a charming, gold-embossed, certificate as a momento. Marguerite also gave a recital at the British Embassy school.

At the conclusion of her scheduled concerts Marguerite had to leave for home because her Philippines visa had run out. Martin Walford in London and Andrew Kyle in Manila confirmed that arrangements had been made for Marguerite to travel to London via Singapore.

In London, her staff, Maria (Portuguese), Carmen (Spanish), Victoria (English), and even her hairdresser, Inger, (Danish), made preparations for the expected home coming.

Marguerite began to pack her bags.

That evening a message from India stated that they expected Marguerite the following morning as planned. The cancellations had not arrived in India.

To add to the impossibility of changing the air tickets at such short notice there was the added problem that India required Marguerite to have a visa. This had not been necessary for previous visits. The India tour was now out of the question.

But not to young men like Martin Walford and Andrew Kyle.

Despite being 5000 miles apart they achieved the impossible.

Marguerite arrived in Bombay airport the next day. It was a haven of peace, and a soldier pushed Marguerite's stool and luggage to the Reception area. The usual hectic activity of this airport was absent, the crowds were absent, and so were the tourists. Armed soldiers stood on guard. She was met by officials who took her to the charming apartment where she had stayed on previous visits.

Her first concert was for the well-established 'Time and Talents Club' in Bombay. Marguerite was welcomed at the airport by Honi Dhondy and Mrs. Kapadia, and she stayed at the charming apartment of Mrs. Bilimoria.

After the concert there was a dinner and the Deputy High Commissioner in Bombay, Mr. Percy Norris, sat at Marguerite's right hand and they were talking for about four hours. Mrs. Angela Norris and her daughter, Madeleine, were also present. Addresses were exchanged and it was arranged that they would visit Marguerite in London later in the year.

While in Bombay Marguerite was able to practise on a Steinway piano for many hours each day in the apartment of Tammy Gazder, herself a chamber musician and known as the Gerald Moore of India. A Bösendorfer piano was tuned in the afternoon and used for the concert in the evening.

The next day Marguerite went shopping with Madames Bilimoria, Dhondy and Gazder, before going to the station to catch the train to Poona. The station is sheer Victoriana, even to

130

We lend our Bosendorfer piano - the cost of transport only charged!

its name, and it was packed with Indian travellers, the second-class passengers boarding their carriages and carrying with them cages, bags, animals, furniture, babies, pots and pans. The lucky ones sat, others stood where they could find space, some hung on the carriage steps, others climbed to the roof. Despite the commotion the elegantly-dressed European lady sitting in a first-class carriage with — of all things — a piano stool, attracted considerable attention!

Even in the first-class there was no air-conditioning. The windows were all open but there were protective bars across them. Otherwise the journey was beautiful, with hills and gentle scenery. When the train puffed its way into Hill Station, Poona, Marguerite alighted with the pushing mass of fellow-passengers but she was immediately recognised by those waiting to meet her because, who but Marguerite Wolff would arrive at Poona railway station with luggage *and* piano stool.

Because Marguerite was so conspicuous in that milling throng on Poona station platform, the secretary of the Poona Music Society, Adi F. Framjee, had no difficulty in recognising her.

The society, whose President is S. L. Kirloskar, keeps the highest standards. Ashkenazi, Ogdon, and Kentner are but three of the great artists who have played there.

Like many people, Marguerite changes her eating habits from time to time. For a period her basic pattern was; egg for breakfast, apple and coffee for lunch, and steak for dinner. At the time of this tour, however, she had changed this slightly and her perfect hosts, Mr. and Mrs. Coombes, with complete urbanity, produced Marguerite's current choice of breakfast, yoghurt and porridge in Poona!

There was a good Steinway for the concert. It was old but Marguerite said, 'it had a soul!' The tuning was very good. She practised from 9.00 a.m. until 1.00 p.m., had a sleep in the afternoon, and then gave her recital to a wonderful audience.

She returned to Bombay en route for the next stop in Calcutta.

The last stop before home was Calcutta. Marguerite was to give a unique concert at the Victoria Memorial, a building designed by Lord Curzon, in the 1920's, in memory of Queen Victoria. Some say it is like the Taj Mahal, others are reminded of St. Paul's Cathedral.

The Durbar Hall, within the Victoria Memorial used for sixty years as a museum, required studied work by the lighting and acoustical technicians in preparing it for its new life as a concert hall.

The green marble platform was carpetted before the piano was put in place, and the lighting was arranged so that the white marble pillars did not cast ugly shadows.

All was ready in time, and Marguerite's recital gave birth to the new identity of this famous old Hall.

132

With all concerts completed as originally planned, Marguerite flew back to London, arriving at 5.45 a.m. . . . to be greeted with the news that her Bombay partner at dinner, Mr. Percy Norris, had been assassinated.

Marguerite Wolff

Victoria Memorial, Seagull Empire and
the Calcutta School of Music
take great pleasure in inviting you
to a piano recital by
British pianist Marguerite Wolff
at the Durbar Hall, Victoria Memorial
on Wednesday 21 November, 7 p.m.

Please show this card at the Southern Gate (Lower Circular Road end) to allow entry into the special car park inside the Victoria Memorial grounds.

ADMIT ONE

Calcutta Invitation Card

©Associated Press Ltd., 1984.

RAJIV GANDHI TAKES OVER FROM HIS MOTHER

©Press Association, 1984.

MR. PERCY NORRIS
Deputy High Commissioner
in Bombay

Marguerite arrived in the Philippines to be told that Mrs. Gandhi had been assassinated. The tour of India was not cancelled, but when Marguerite arrived back in England she was greeted at London Airport with the news that Mr. Percy Norris had been assassinated.

No voice; but oh! the silence sank like music on my heart.

Coleridge. *The Rime of the Ancient Mariner*.

The still, sad music of humanity.

Wordsworth. *Tintern Abbey*.

The headline of a report of Marguerite's playing in Africa was:—

'If Music Be The Food of Love.'

This quotation from Shakespeare's *Twelfth Night* continues with an entreating two words:—

'Play On!'

Index

Selected list

Illustrations indicated by bold type

f = footnote

Aaronovitch, Izzy 15
Aronowitz, Cecil 96
Albeniz 37
Albert Hall, The 43-46, 48-51, 54, 56, 59, 60, 70, 71, **124**
Aquino, Benigno 127
Arango, Jaramillo 'Jaime', Dr. (17.1.1897) 64, **65**
Ashkenazy, Vladimir 107, 115, 130, 132
Azulay, Gertrude 16-27, 29, 41

Bach 19, 76, 109, 123
Bacon, Francis 116
Baker, Josephine 39, 40
Bantock, Sir Granville 21, 23
Barbirolli, Sir John 22, 27, 44, 128
Barron, Mr. 11-16, 19
Bartok, Bela 92
Basch, Mrs. 54, 63
Bauer, Harold 109
B.B.C. 49, 50, 128
Bechstein 110
Beethoven 19, 22, 46, 49, 57, 96, 110, 119, 121, 123, 124
Bell, Ivy 16
Benzi, Roberto **72**
Berg, Alban 43
Berkovitz, George 92
Berlioz 38, 94
Bernstein, Leonard 56
Bilimoria, Mrs. 130
Bliss, Sir Arthur 82-99, **85, 87**, 102, 113, 117
Bliss, Lady Gertrude 81, 84, 89, 99
Bliss, Kennard 93
Blüthner f109, 110, 121
Bösendorfer 109, 110, 130, **131**
Boult, Sir Adrian 95
Brahms 19-21, 23, 54, 56-59, 68, 119, 121, 123, 124
Brendel, Alfred 115
Bridge, Frank 113
Bridgewater, Leslie 44
Broadwood 110
Buckley, Lady **103**
Buckley, Sir John 116
Bush, Alan 62
Busoni 86

Cagnoni, Romano 97
Callas, Maria 51
Camden, Archie **61**
Campbell, Judge 73
Campbell, Miss 80
Campoli 44, 54
Cardin, Pierre 35
Carmen, 129
Catley, Gwen 54
Central Hall (Westminster) 44
Chamberlain, Neville 72
Chanel 35
Ching, James 32
Chopin 19, 37, 38, 54, 90, 96, 98, 114, 116, 119, 121
Christie, Winifred 109
Churchill 21, 94
Clidat, France 115
Collet, Robert 87, 115
Cook, Gladys 29, 30
Coombes, Mr. and Mrs. 132
Cooper, Lady Diana 34-37, 40
Cooper, Duff (Viscount Norwich) 36
Corredi, Nelly 50
Cortot 24
Covent Garden (Royal Opera House) 49, 50, 68
Cowley, Ondine 125, 128
Creighton, Ursula 86
Cristofori 110
Crowson, Lamar 96
Curzon, Clifford 72
Curzon, Lord 132
Czerny 19

Dale, Sir William 72, 75
Dalldorf, Charles 114
Dalldorf, Mrs. 114
Daunton, Frank 115
Davis, Peter 84
Debussy 37
Denison, Michael 51
Dhondy, Honi 130
Dikko 123
Dior 35
Dolmetsch 62
Dorothea (nanny) **80**
Dugarde, Harry 72

Dukes, Ashley 8
Duncan, Raymond 38-40
Duncan (see Isadora)
Dyll, Felix Van 30

Earhart, Amelia 12
Elgar 49, 93, 94, 113
Ellenburg, David 62, 63
Ellerup, Athe **123**
Ellinson, Iso 43
Elizabeth, the Queen Mother **101**
Elton, Howard **71**
Erard 110
Esther (Aunt Essie) 34
Esther, Queen 36
Eva (aunt) 44
Evans, Nancy 15

Fagan, Keith 97, 98, 126
Faraday, Derek 88
Farmer, Geoffrey 42
Fauré 92, 95
Fleming, Ian 72
Flesch, Carl 30
Foggin, Myers 112, 113
Forsdyke, Sir John 62, 63
Foster, John 98
Fragonard 90
Framjee, Adi F. 132
Franck, César 30, 33, 124
Freccia, Massino, **103**

Galsworthy, Sir John 116
Galsworthy, Lady 116, 117
Galtat, Claude 37
Gandhi, Mrs. 127, **134**
Gazder, Tammy 130
Gestapo 40
Gigli 52
Gladstone 21
Glazebrook, Robert 111
Gloucester, Duke of **103**
Gobbi, Tilde 45, 46
Gobbi, Tito 43, 45, 46, 48-51, **53**
Godfrey, Admiral John 72, 75
Goehr, Walter **75**
Goering, Field Marshall 40
Goodman, Violet 44

Goossens, Leon 54, **61**, 93
Graça, Fernando Lopes 98
Graeme, Peter 95
Gray, Dulcie 51
Grayson, Eunice **61**
Greenhouse-Allt, Dr. 22
Gregory, Paul 115
Grieg 123
Groves, Olive 44
Gus, Brother 129

Hallé Orchestra 44, 52
Hamburg, Mark 22
Harcourt, Lady 58
Hartnell, Norman 34, **35**
Harrison, Sydney 32
Harrison, Vernon 115
Haydn 62, 98, 124
Heifitz 43
Hemmink, Wim 100, 102
Hermann, Freddie 30, 31, 33, 41, 42
Hess, Myra 15
Hillman (artist) 27-29
Hochhauser, Victor 30, 42
Holt, Harold 44
Horatio (driver) **123**
Horrowitz 43, 112
Hubbersgilt, Monty 54-60, 71-73
Huddersfield Choral Society 52
Hurwitz, Emanuel 96
Huttenbach, Trudy 109

Ibbs and Tillett 43, 95
Imperial Concert Agency (I.C.A.) 29, 30
Inger (Hairdresser) 129
Isadora (Duncan) 38, 39

Jacob, Gordon 17, f17
Joel, John 42-45, **44**, 58, 72
Johansen, Gunnar 115
Johnson, Amy 12
Johnson, Bill 54
Jolliffe, Sir Anthony 101
Jones, Howard 17
Joyce, Eileen 44

Kapadia, Mrs. 130
Karbos, Alona 30
Kardré, Mr. 34
Katovska, Adella 30
Kentner, Griselda 30
Kentner, Louis 30-33, **31**, 37, 41, 42, 46, 48, 54, 56-60, **58, 65**, 71, 72, 84, 86, 96, **114**, 115, 132
King Thea 95
Kirloskar, S. L. 132
Knott, Thomas 16, 19

Kodály 92
Kosky Cynthia 119, 120
Kosky John 119
Kosky Nat **119, 120**, 119-121
Kurtz, Arved **112**, 113
Kurtz, Edmund 112
Kurtz, Efrem 112
Kurtz, Susie 112
Kustow, Mrs. L. 115
Kutner (Solomon) 28
Kyle, Andrew 129, 130

Lambert, Sir Anthony 113
Lampe, Oscar 43
Landau, Mabel 16
Laroche 35
Lawson, Solly 62
Lebell, Ludwig 15, 23, 24, 40
Lee, Jo E. 29
Legge, Walter 15
Leoncavallo 43, 49
Levinskaya, Madame 16
Lily (aunt) 59
Lindsay-Finn, Sir Basil 107
Lindsay-Finn, Lady 107
Liszt 30, 37, 38, 42, 54, 90, 96-98, 114, 116, 123, 126
Liszt Society, The 96, 106, 114, 115, 119
Locke, Josef 54
Lollobrigida, Gina 51
London Philharmonic Orchestra 128
London Symphony Orchestra 33-36, 42, 56, 58, 70, 72, 98
Londonderry, The Lord 115
Louise, Princess 108
Lovelock, William 37, 98
Lynford and Joel 42-60, 71, 72
Lynford, Mark 42, 44

Macnab, Crystal 72, 75, 115
Macnab, George 57, 72, 75
Magnani, Anna 51
Mamo, Sir Anthony 89
Mamo, Lady 84, 89
Marcos, Madame 127, 129
Maria (maid) 81
Marland, Frederic 129
Mathieson, Muir 43, 46
Matthay, Tobias 32
Maurois, André 7
Mayerl, Billy 44
McMahon, Ivor 96
Melos Ensemble 95, 96
Mendelssohn 94, 96, 119, 121
Menuhin, Diana 30
Menuhin, Yehudi 30, 32, 115
Merrick, Paul 115
Midgeley, Walter 44
Milton 8

Mistarz, Eunice 115
Moiseiwitsch, Benno 21, 22, 93
Moór, Emanuel 108, 109
Moore, Gerald 51, 130
Moss, Mrs. (Derrick's mother) 68, **104**
Moss, Albert 70, 82
Moss, Eileen 70
Moss, Lewis 70, **71**, 72, 73, 82
Moss, Lily **71**
Moss, Grandpa **71, 103**
Mozart 7, 62, 90, 96, **110**, 123, 126

New York Philharmonic Orchestra 56
Newton, Ivor 51
Newton-Wood, Noel 86
Nichols, Robert 93
Norris, Angela 130
Norris, Madeleine 130
Norris, Percy 130, 133, **134**
Northern Philharmonic Orchestra 49
Novello, Ivor 9

Offenbach 38
Ogdon, John 107, 132
Orbegoso, Karyna de 118, 119

Palestine Symphony Orchestra 44
Parikian, Manoug 23
Paris 23, 24, 34-41, 52, 59, 61, 68
Patou 35
Paul, Alan 115
Percival, Alice 110
Peyer, Gervase de 95, 96
Pleyel 110
Price, Ann (Norman Hartnell) 35
Pumphries, Nigel **38**

Rachmaninoff Sergei 93
Raevsky, Artemy 74, f74
Raybould, Clarence 49, 52
Rayne, Lord 115
Reliable (driver) 123
Révillon 35
Richards, Ivor 112
Riddick, Kathleen 75
Robeson, Paul 42
Rodwell, Edward 120
Rodwell, Shirley 81
Rodzinski, Artur **55**, 56, 57
Roper, Stanley 21
Rosenwald, Mary 112
Rossini 43
Rothschild, Mrs. Lionel de 72
Rowley, Alec 123
Royal Philharmonic Orchestra 43, 46, 98
Rubinstein 21
Ruffle, Mrs. Trudy 107

Saint-Laurent 35
Saint-Saëns 124
Sargent, Sir Malcolm 125
Satie 38
Scarlatti 95
Schenker (photographer) 27
Schmitt 19, 20
Schnabel, Arthur 32, 43
Schouvaloff, Anna 73
Schubert 39, 57, 58, 94, 96, 98, 109, 119, 126
Schumann 20, 37, 98, 114, 123
Schwarzkopf, Elisabeth 51, 68
Scott, Sidney 112
Scott-Fox, Sir David 89
Scott-Fox, Lady 89
Segal, Lord **101**
Sellick, Phyllis 43
Shakespeare 7, 63, 110, 134
Sherriff, Paul 73
Sherriff, Alexander 74
Shuard, Amy 51
Sibelius 89
Silveri, Paolo 49, **50**, 52, 68
Sinclair, Joyce 61
Sitwell, Sir Sacheverell 115
Slade, Justice 72
Smith, Cyril 43
Snelling, Mr. 119
Solomon 24, 28, 29, 64, 93, 95
Solti, Sir Georg 115
Souter, Kenneth 115
Spenser, Edmund 90
Srawley, Christopher 115
Stebbing, Professor 21
Stein 110
Steinway (pianos) 88, 105, 108, 110-112, 114, 121, 132
Stewart, Michael 113
Stokowski, Leopold 56
Stratton, George 58, 98
Strauss, Johann 37

Sunday, Billy 39
Swarbi, Mr. 132
Sylvester (driver) 123
Szmanowski, Karol 119

Tangye, Nigel 12
Tate, Dorothy 89, 90
Tate, Muriel 89, 90
Tausky, Vilem 126
Tessler, Heather **71**
Timms, Eirik 121, 122, **122**
Timms, Richard 121, 122
Toye, Wendy **61**
Trinity College of Music 15, 21-24, 28, 34, 37, 41, 42, 44, 51, 112, 128
Tripp, Mr. and Mrs. **127**
Trotman, Anne 29
Tschaikovsky 59, 61, 70, 71, 75, 123
Tuck, Lady 70
Turina, Joaquin 76

Vaughan, Reginald 72
Vaughan Williams, Mrs. 89
Vecchi, Joseph 48
Ver, General Fabian 127
Verdi 43, 51
Victoria, Queen 133
Victoria (staff) 129

Wagner 39, 92
Wales, Diana, Princess of 125
Walford, Arthur, **71**
Walford, Charles 105
Walford, Martin 129, 130
Walford, Penelope, **71**
Walsh, John 112, 113
Walter, Bruno 56
Walton, William 30
Weil, Terence 96
Weston, John 108
Whittaker, Roger 120
Wigmore Hall 33, 44, 45, 72, 76, 81

Wilhelm, Kaiser 108
Williams, Adrian 114, 115
Wilson, Cecil 72
Winchelsea, Countess 72, 75
Windsor, Duke and Duchess of 38
Wingate, Angela (née) **91**
Wingate, Jonathan **91**
Wingate, Roger **91**
Winter Gardens (Drury Lane) 57
Wolff, Alber 39
Wolff, Marguerite (family)
  Nina (mother) **11**-18, 21, 22, **26**, 39, 44, 48, 62, 68, 70, **71**
  Walter (father) 11, **12**, 13, 16, 21, 22, **26**, 48, **71**
  Adolph (brother) 11, 12, **13**, 16
  Arthur (brother) 11, 12, **13**
  Dolly (Dorothy, sister) 11, 12, **14**, 15-18, 21, 22, 24, 27, 30, 33, 34, 41, 42, 58, 59, 62, 65, **71**, 81, **91**, 92, 110
  Derrick (Moss, husband) 59-61, 68, **69**, 70, **71**, 73, 76, 93, 99, **102**, 112
  Crystal (daughter) 74, 76, **79**, 80, 82, **83**, 84, **92**, 94, **103**, **104**, **125**, **128**
  Gloria (daughter) 74, **79**, **80**, 82, 83, 84, 92, **93**, 94, **103**, **104**, 129
  Marguerite (pictures) **9**, **14**, **37**, **38**, **47**, **50**, **61**, **64**, **69**, **71**, **76**, **77**, **78**, **80**, **87**, **94**, **97**, **103**, **104**, **106**, **123**, **124**, **126**, **127**, **128**
Wood, Sir Henry 15
Woodland, Rae 96
Wren Orchestra 126
Wyck, Wilfred Van 117, 119

Yorkshire Evening Post 49, 51, 52
Yorkshire Symphony Orchestra 52
Young, Emanuel 62
Ysaye 86

Zaid, Prince 34